HALF THE HOUSE

My Life In and Out of Jerusalem

"This is a beautiful, deeply stirring memoir about breaking away from Jerusalem and also about discovering Jerusalem. Perhaps all coming of age stories are about loss, exile, and the ambiguity of return, but when the story unfolds against the backdrop of Jerusalem, it reverberates in large and mysterious ways. Especially when it is written with the eye of a poet, the insight of a psychologist, and a heart of wisdom."
    —Jonathan Rosen, author of *The Talmud and the Internet*

"*Half the House* is the tale of a woman's odyssey to accommodate the spiritual mysteries of her birthplace (Jerusalem) and the intellectual freedoms of her adopted city (New York). Rachel Berghash shows how, in a life long struggle to be faithful to both, she made them one. An evocative and engaging memoir."
    —Clinton Bailey, author of *Bedouin Poetry from Sinai and the Negev.*

"A beautiful book. One feels life from the inside, yet feasts on sensory realities, sights and sounds of Jerusalem and New York. At once spiritual and down to earth, combining everyday with spiritual needs. A book to be savored in its unhurried charting of change, loss, the yet-to-be, while drawing on an abiding presence of the past. A deep affirmation of the human condition, expressed with sensitivity and care, a poetic and healing sense of time melding with something that endures."
    —Michael Eigen, author of *Contact with the Depths*, *The Sensitive Self*,
    and *Madness and Murder*

"The author's ongoing, unique ties between New York and Jerusalem reflect the story of her life, one that has come full circle. Her poetic prose dreams of a Jerusalem that was and could perhaps be revived one day, and of peace and hope for true human relations between Jews and Arabs. Required reading for anyone who wishes to understand and sense the soul of Jerusalem."
    —Ari Rath, former editor of *The Jerusalem Post*

RACHEL BERGHASH

HALF THE HOUSE

My Life In and Out of Jerusalem

SANTA FE

Sunstone books may be purchased for educational, business, or sales
promotional use. For information please write: Special Markets Department,
Sunstone Press, P.O. Box 2321, Santa Fe, New Mexico 87504-2321.

Body typeface › Palatino
Printed on acid free paper

Library of Congress Cataloging-in-Publication Data

Berghash, Rachel, 1935–
    Half the house : my life in and out of Jerusalem / Rachel Berghash.
        p. cm.
    Includes bibliographical references.
    ISBN 978-0-86534-805-9 (softcover : alk. paper)
    1. Berghash, Rachel, 1935- 2. Israelis--New York (State)--New York--Biography.
3. Jews--New York (State)--New York--Biography. 4. Jews--Jerusalem--Biography.
5. Jerusalem--Biography. I. Title.
    F128.9.J5B43973 2011
    305.892'407471092--dc22
    [B]
                                    2011011394

Published in

WWW.SUNSTONEPRESS.COM
SUNSTONE PRESS / POST OFFICE BOX 2321 / SANTA FE, NM 87504-2321 /USA
(505) 988-4418 / ORDERS ONLY (800) 243-5644 / FAX (505) 988-1025

To Mark, husband and friend

He who hopes to grow in spirit
will have to transcend obedience and respect.
He'll hold to some laws
but he'll mostly violate
both law and custom, and go beyond
the established, inadequate norm. . . .
He won't be afraid of the destructive act:
half the house will have to come down. . . .

From "Growing in Spirit"
—C.P. Cavafy

Contents

Overture

TERROR AND ICE CREAM

Corpses are thrown here, says my father, pointing to a valley in the Jerusalem forest as we drive by. My father exaggerates what he reads in the newspapers. His voice is uneasy. It is this new bad element in the city, these mobsters, who dispose of their victims in this valley, my father adds. The stars shimmer in a July sky, and the air is cool and crisp. I sit in the backseat with my mother. My father is in the front next to my husband, who is at the wheel. Mobsters in Jerusalem, throwing corpses into a valley? I don't believe it. Yet the words slowly penetrate me and fill me with terror.

I have known this terror since childhood. It doesn't surface often, but when it does it has an ominous impact on me. As when I once, spontaneously, turned off the lights on a Sabbath Eve, breaking Jewish law, and was suddenly seized with a formless terror of some unknown force that made me feel powerless, as if the life were drained out of me. And later, on one of my summer visits to Jerusalem from New York, while driving in a car on the Sabbath, my father's admonishments echo: I am violating a holy space, desecrating not only the Sabbath, but contaminating the purity of this city. I am causing pain not only to my father, my mother, and God, but by driving in a car that sails through the sanctified, almost traffic-free streets, I am responsible for transforming Jerusalem into a mundane, secular, temporal place.

After having moved to New York, after having abandoned, almost completely, the practice of religious observances, I can hear my mother's voice: A sin, she would say, if I told her that I ride the subway on the Sabbath. She would say that about my other transgressions, such as blowing out the Sabbath candles. (Before leaving the house I'd blow out the candles for fear they would cause a fire.) I could hear my mother pronouncing the word *sin* in an annihilating voice. Whenever I hear it, even from a great distance, I lie down, feeling barely alive. Lie down as

I once did, on the grass by a river, terrified to disobey my parents, who have instructed me not to go rowing in a boat with my friends lest the boat capsize and I drown. I saw my friends rowing, rowing away, and I lay on my stomach writhing in pain.

At home, my mother monitored me, watched my every step. When I was fourteen, a boy in class asked me to be his girlfriend. I blushed, and said, Yes. Once a week, he invited me to go to the movies with him, and in late afternoons he came to pick me up. The boys in our school had to wear yarmulkes, but Tzvi, when not in school, took his off. He stood downstairs in front of my house, whistling "our" whistle, and my mother came out on the terrace to take a look. Seeing him bareheaded, she grimaced. Upon my return from the movies, she said in an angry voice, Why isn't he wearing a yarmulke? Her voice was sharp, she didn't expect an answer, nor did the question mean I should stop seeing Tzvi. Perhaps it was her indirect way of inculcating guilt and fear in me, her way of releasing anxiety. Perhaps she was repeating a pattern begun as a child, noticing how her older brother adhered to Jewish law, rigidly.

My mother expresses her pain about me abandoning the practice of Jewish law, and paradoxically denies that I have done so. I fear her imminent remarks: On Friday mornings, when I call from New York to wish her a good Sabbath, she says, You probably have already finished cooking for the Sabbath. Though I would admit to not having cooked for the Sabbath, implying that I might break Jewish law and do so during the night and the day of rest, I feel like a little girl who must submit to her.

My obedience is a matter of habit. Often, when I disobeyed my parents, I feared abandonment, annihilation, not being well thought of. My parents and God—are they the same? Did they merge in my mind? I think of God as possibility, without which I wouldn't know there is something more satisfying than my present state. Perhaps my terror has very little to do with my parents or with God. I need to take responsibility for my terror and my anxiety. It would take me many years to acknowledge that I am anxious, and to discover that anxiety is harmful, a kind of a sin: to feel that I deserve God's forgiveness for what *I* think of as my sins, and to genuinely ask His forgiveness for them.

And it would take many more years to understand the full meaning of a poem by C.P. Cavafy:

> He who hopes to grow in spirit
> will have to transcend obedience and respect.
> He'll hold to some laws
> but he'll mostly violate
> both law and custom, and go beyond
> the established, inadequate norm. . . .
> He won't be afraid of the destructive act:
> half the house will have to come down[1]

I want to do away with customs, with obedience, with respect for the law. But I fear the destructive act, my own aggression. I fear the house will come down. As I go my own way, having my own thoughts, there is still a voice that forbids the spontaneous word, lest the ground drop out from beneath me and leave me suspended in the air without the law and the rules to hold onto. As I am engaged in thinking, I fear violating both law and custom, disobeying the strict, forbidding, exacting, punishing voice. As I lead my own life, I fear going beyond the established norm even though the norm is inadequate, even though it confines me. I fear surrendering to the great unknown, of "becoming what I had not yet been," as Yeats would say. But the pull to break through persists. Another voice beckons me, summons me to glimpse an endlessly expansive world. And a conflict widens, like the gorge in west Jerusalem, very close to Mount Herzl, near my parents' house; it is forever widening, ready to consume, to swallow. I bend, prostrate, kneel. I am still the little girl looking for Mother's and Father's approval.

On a trip to Canada with my husband and two sons one summer, we decide to go on a ski lift to see the view from Mont Tremblant, which is opposite us. I must sit on the chairlift quickly or I will miss it. I am shocked at how fast it goes up with just a bar to hold on to. I look at the valley below, the abyss, the vast world; my legs dangle above the abyss. Any wrong move, any inadvertent move, and I will fall. Any move my sons will make, they will fall. I ask my older son, who sits next to me, if he is afraid, and he says No; I turn back and ask my husband and my younger son whether they are afraid, and they say No; it is peculiar then to be afraid, I think. We are going up; the ascent will never end. When we finally land on the mountain, I say, I am not going back that way, my legs dangling in the air is too frightening, I am going down by foot. My husband says, This is crazy, you will sit next to me this time. But the children, I say. They will sit by themselves, he says. Impossible, I say. He says, They'll be fine. And I am up on the chairlift, I am sitting next to my husband this time, the children sit behind us. We are going down, and I am terrified, and I begin to sob, I sob loudly, I sob uncontrollably, I sob hard, everything in me sobs, my tensions, my worries, my anxiety over my children, my fear of my parents, fears I have about doing the wrong thing, everything sobs, I will fall into the abyss and die, my last and final fall; there is no world, there is no "I." My terror, my sobbing, and me are one. There is nothing else.

My mother believed in my doing what satisfies me. She gave me room to be. She permitted my feelings of grief and fear, as well as desire. In her presence I feel at ease when I cry. She never tells me to stop. Once, in the kitchen, I cried when she told me something—I don't remember whether it was about someone's misfortune or someone's kindness—and she said, Cry, cry, this is something to cry about. From the time I was two years old, my mother arranged for the neighbors' children to come and play with me. She wanted me to have friends. She permitted me to stay home on days I didn't feel like going to school: You don't exploit anybody, you are straight as a ruler, she said, and you are not greedy. She and my father did not interfere with the way I dressed. My father, only on one occasion, at the age of eighteen, reproved me for wearing black stockings, saying whores wear black stockings. My parents rarely criticized my boyfriends; they made no rules as to when I should be back home from a date.

When my parents thought they were indulging me, they called me *Basichidke,* which means "only child." It's an endearing term and it meant that they cherished me. However, I wanted to have a sibling. I kept looking at my mother's belly, and I imagined it growing bigger. If only I could have an older brother who would bring home his friends, and they would surround me, and I would pick and choose whomever I wanted as a boyfriend. I didn't feel my parents spoiled me, though I often felt thwarted by my mother's over-attentiveness. In winter, she bought me leather boots to keep my feet warm. I wanted rubber boots, the kind my friends wore. But rubber boots do not protect the feet from the cold weather, my mother insisted. Later, when I read Rilke's "Prodigal Son," I thought of how similar our experiences have been: upon returning home from roaming in the fields, the son is led over to a table in front of a lamp, and the light falls on him alone, while the others stayed in shadow. I lamented with him not having the right to the slightest danger, and having to promise a hundred times not to die. The son is a creature that belongs to his family; they had long ago fashioned a life for him "out of his small past and their own desires . . ." standing "day and night under the influence of their love, between their hope and their mistrust, before their approval or their blame. . . ."[2] In the fields, though, he can be whatever he wants to be, nothing but a bird if he wants to, without being concerned that he is giving pleasure or pain by what he is doing. He wants the freedom he encounters in the fields, where "none of this became fate, and the sky passed over him as over nature. . . ."[3] He wants a humble love that does not burden him, a love without the anxiety that contaminates it. This is the kind of love I experience when I am in a room writing or reading, and my husband is in another, or sometimes we are in the same room as we attend to whatever we are doing, privately, silently, and the house is quiet, all is still. We talk to each other but mostly we are silent. There is a security of being loved and loving, and a trust that helps me to be true to myself, no longer terrified to be my own person.

I've experienced similar moments with my father. For all his reproaching me and agreeing with my mother about my religious transgressions, my father was more relaxed than she was in the way he practiced his religion. I took him for granted. Yet I trusted him. The few bad fights I've had with him were honest, straightforward fights. Once, as a teenager, during dinner, I became so mad at him I threw a knife across the table. Another time when my father asked that I take the garbage downstairs, I said, No, I'm afraid of the cats, they jump at me from the garbage bin, shrieking. You are spoiled, my father said, and slapped my arm; the metal band of my watch opened and scratched my hand, which bled. I was indignant and I cried, but secretly I thought I deserved it.

My father once said that had he lived in America, he would have joined a Conservative synagogue where men and women sit together, not separated by a *mechitza*. When I was ten, I went with him to Tel Aviv. We sat in a café on the beach and had ice cream. It was a hot day, but a canopy shaded our table. There was just the right amount of space between my father and me. I could just be. Away from the city, which has been burdened with an oppressive past, evident in the history-laden alleys that had made their mark on my father's determined yet hesitant gait, my father was relaxed. His eyes, which were weary most of the time, seemed calm. A light breeze came from the ocean. The waves splashed the shore. My father's head was bare. He had no hat or yarmulke. I asked him why, and he said, In Jerusalem, one must cover one's head, but here in Tel Aviv it's different. The remark came as a pleasant surprise. I liked my father for not sticking to rigid rules, being the way he was in Tel Aviv, unburdened, without a hat.

PART I

1

WALKS WITH MY FATHER

There are buildings in Jerusalem that remind me of my father's life—among them the orphanage he was sent to as a young teenager. Whenever I've walked by that orphanage I turn my head away. It must have been terrible to live in a place where everyone is an orphan and the food rationed, to be bereft of a father who died a sudden death on a street in Istanbul, on his way to Poland, where he went to ask his family for financial help, and to have a mother who was destitute, whose property was stolen by a relative. (My grandmother would curse this relative till the end of her life.) While living in the orphanage my father once walked to his mother's house and stood by the back windows waving to her; she did not wave back. I do not love my mother, he would say matter-of-factly, not without emotion, but without an apology or an explanation.

Contrary to my thinking, my father remembered enjoying the two years he spent in the orphanage after his father died. While there he fell in love with the principal's daughter. He seems to have kept her image inside him; when he mentions her, a satisfied smile spreads on his face. The principal favored him and gave him the lead role of Mordecai in a Purim play. When he left the orphanage my father began working to support his mother and his two sisters; he did not have the opportunity to attend a yeshiva, which most children his age, born in Jerusalem at the time, did. But until the end of his life my father remembered his privileged position at the orphanage, and he supported it, a tradition my husband and I and other relatives have continued. During my walks with my father, I do not tire of noticing how he knows his way around Jerusalem; nothing is foreign to him. We walk through the city park. In its midst is Mamila Pool, an abandoned pool, something of an anomaly. The park has only a few trees, and sadness permeates the place. The name, Mamila, has an ebullient ring to it. Before the War of Independence Mamila was a busy neighborhood with many stores, and I would go there with my mother to buy dress fabric. After the war, the buildings are partially destroyed, there is no glass in the windows, the entrances to stores are doorless. Across the street, anti-sniper walls separate the Old City from the new.

My father likes to explain to me the geography of Jerusalem. He points to the north and says, This is Nabi Samuel where the prophet Samuel is buried. I am curious about why the name is in Arabic, but I don't ask, and my father doesn't explain. The site is remote, surrounded by bare hills. Whenever we go there a strong wind blows. I think it is the prophet's restless spirit.

My father also likes to explain to me the names and locations of the gates surrounding the Old City of Jerusalem. He was born there and talks about these gates with ease. I admire him for his knowledge but I think it is very odd to comfortably utter a name like Dung Gate. I also find it odd that a gate is called Sha'ar Harachamim, which means Gate of Mercy. I imagine the gate to be a resting place for the weary.

He points in the direction of Jaffa Gate at the entrance of the Old City, as the spot where Kaiser Franz Josef, the Austro-Hungarian monarch, entered the city. He remembers being told of that day as a day of honor, dignity, excitement. That the Kaiser himself chose to come to the Holy Land, the poor land, subjugated to the Ottoman Empire: that the people had a chance to see him "with their own eyes."

My father also points to the windmill on a small hill above Mamila. What is it doing there? Is it real? Agnon, in one of his stories, populates the windmill with demons, and though I don't believe in demons I don't go very close to the place. Still further is the Terra Sancta building, owned by the Franciscan Custodians of the Latin Holy Places, part of which is rented by the Hebrew University. The Madonna sculpture on top of the building is in charge, sustaining the original Christian spirit of the building. It is disconcerting to me that the university inhabits a Christian place. Whether this is because it taints Jewish law, or because it conflicts with the Christian identity of the place, I cannot say. My feelings are unclear to me.

Sometimes my father and I walk to the caves of the Sanhedrin. The caves are in the north. They are secretive and forbidding. I revere them. I imagine their openings to be like God's ears. The mysterious darkness as I peek inside, the natural structure of each cave, beckons me. Years later, I would be astonished to learn that caves live and die, that rocks have feelings, and that trees repair their damaged branches. I think that life in a cave is benign, safe. In a cave one can glimpse the divine, as in Mayan caves, where it was believed that rain started and then went up, reaching deities in the sky.

Next to the caves of the Sanhedrin and the zoo, which I like to visit, is the cave of Shimon Hatzaddik, the righteous man. On the holiday Lag B'Omer (commemorating, among other things, the heroism of Bar-Kochba in his revolt against the Roman Empire), everyone flocks there. The Sephardic Jews, accompanied by their children, bring food and have a picnic. The place becomes noisy and littered. The Ashkenazi Jews remark, We don't do that, that is a Sephardic custom. In the field across from our house my friends and I light a bonfire, as is the custom. The ascending flames commemorate Bar-Kochba's valiant revolt against the Romans. I would like to have met Bar-Kochba. Though he lost the war to the Romans, he is remembered as a great hero.

On one of my yearly summer visits to Jerusalem I visit the neighborhood of my father's store. To the west of the store is the Russian compound where the Russian Orthodox church stands. Once, my husband, accompanied by my father and me, came to the Russian compound to ask permission from the Russian Orthodox Church to photograph nuns in the convent in Ein Karem for one of his photographic projects. My father knew the way; he led us through the entrance, a long corridor full of shadows, to the bishop's office. He moved quickly, assuredly. He was at home. In the same way, he was at home when visiting an Arab family in Ramallah before the Independence War, or when visiting his old Arab customers in the Old City after the 1967 war. He was equally at home dealing with Arabs and with Christians. When he sold my piano after I left the country to two monks from the Old City, he said, The monks didn't haggle about the price. Christians never do.

My father takes me on adventures. I go with him and his four male friends to Jericho and to Elisha's spring nearby, an hour away from Jerusalem. I sit by the spring and look at the water. According to the biblical story the water in Jericho was foul, causing miscarriages; Elisha made it wholesome by filling a new bowl with salt and throwing the salt into the spring, the source of the water. I believe the water is holy. I am lulled by its rhythm. I become part of the water, the still sky, the amiable palm trees. On another day, a sunny afternoon, I dance with my father on our street. Arms around each other, we dance as we sing: *Yamina, Yamina* (right, right), we turn to the right; *smola, smola* (left, left), *lefanim* (forward), *ahora* (back). It is summer. The street is empty. My father is without a care. When we visit the Church of the Nativity in Bethlehem my father and I enter through a very small door. The church is half dark. My father points to the lit candles and the singing chorus and says, Look how beautiful it is. His face is calm and his eyes restful. I am holding his hand; it's quiet and warm.

A special treat is the visit to the Cave of the Machpelah in Hebron. It is astonishing that Abraham, Sara, Isaac, Rebekkah, Leah, and Jacob are all buried there—all in one place. I want to pray to one of the fathers and mothers, but the many tombs confuse me. My father reassures me: Surely, you could pray to all of them. But I still prefer praying at Rachel's tomb, buried on a lonely road between Jerusalem and Bethlehem. The tomb is housed in a small building facing a bare field. In a dark and small room, Rachel's soul lies hidden in the walls, deserted.

Whenever we have a rainless season in the winter, my father worries about a drought. His community believes that a drought is decreed from heaven because of some grave communal sin, and it fasts and prays to avert it. Would these prayers affect nature, stubborn as it is? I have my doubts. And yet I love and am humbled by the brief daily prayers for rain and dew.

My father tells me about the locusts that invaded Palestine in 1915, destroying the crops. There was a famine after the locusts' invasion, and a famine after the British had occupied the Old City. My father would follow the British soldiers, picking up orange peels they discarded and eating them. Often the skin around his elbows turns red with a rash; it seems to me the rash is a remnant from the time he was hungry and the city was wasted by famine. I am frightened by the mention of the word locusts, perhaps because it is one of the ten plagues that had hit Egypt, or because of the image I have of a mass of insects descending on our city, hurling itself at the city as Hosea prophesied, wounding the few trees in our neighborhood, leaving them bare, or sweeping through the trees in the outskirts of the city, making them white and dry.

I imagine the locusts as a dark cloud over the Old City when my father was a child—women standing in courtyards looking troubled, whispering to each other, men fasting, gathering in synagogues or outside synagogues, sounding the ram's horn, praying to avert the decree. I imagine the men in the Old City praying, like the groups of men in my neighborhood. They recite the "Sanctification of the Moon" at the conclusion of the Sabbath, huddled under the sky, looking upward at the slender new moon as it sheds a faint light on them. Later I would learn, to my surprise, that locusts are edible, that John the Baptist ate locusts and wild honey in the rugged Judean Hills where he made his home.

My grandmother's neighborhood, Mazkeret Moshe, was built by Moses Montefiori, a wealthy Jew, in the late 19th century. It is one of the first neighborhoods built outside the walls of the Old City. My grandmother lived in her house with my two aunts. The house had two rooms: a front room and a bedroom. The front room was for eating. It contained crudely made furniture: a table and chairs, a small sofa, and a cabinet for dishes and food. The bedroom, a large room in the back, had beds and a wardrobe for clothes. The kitchen and the bathroom were in the courtyard. My aunts preferred to meet their dates, arranged by a matchmaker, at our more comfortable home. They were inseparable, very attached to each other and to their mother, perhaps due to the history of the family, which like so many other families in the Old City of Jerusalem, was marked by separation, illnesses, and early deaths. One of my father's great-grandmother's sons left for South Africa, and she never saw him again. As my father tells me how she wept for her son every day, he, too, wells up with tears.

The older of the two aunts was delicate, vulnerable, a Tennessee Williams Blanche type with an uncertain manner suggesting a moth. I sensed the commotion around her. She was shadowy, half-hidden in a ghostly silence, and she caused my parents extreme worry. Before having a date she would stand in front of the mirror. I would watch her turn sideways and backwards to check her figure. I would watch the meticulous way she put lipstick on, or powdered her face, the way she would rinse a dish with great caution, the way she held brittle things—a teacup, a vase—the way she protected herself from dust and disappointments. At night, as I lay in bed, I prayed for my aunts to marry. Marrying was supposed to be the solution. The night my aunt introduced me to her fiancé she was indeed like a moth: hesitant, fluttery. Infatuated with him, she seemed on the "threshold of happiness." Six months after she married, her husband divorced her, complaining that she suffered from "nerves": she would spread butter on two sides of the bread and commit other sins of frailty that remain unknown to me. After the divorce she moved in with us. A year later she died. My mother told me she was run over by a car while crossing the street. My father, though bent to the inevitable, the indifferent world around him, sometimes wept. On the occasion of his sister's divorce and at the time he identified her dead body, he wept all night.

Years later, in 1990, I visit my grandmother's neighborhood, which has become a lure for artists. The small houses and the oblong-shaped, treeless area in its center now look quaint. Some of the doors of the shabby houses are painted with bright colors, and the few trees seem greener than in the past. A tall, wooden gate now hides my grandmother's small house. I recall visiting my grandmother on the Sabbath. She seemed indifferent to what I did and what I thought, and that was comforting. She made me something to eat, and I sat in her house and dreamt my dreams. Though my grandmother grew up in the Old City of Jerusalem she never learned to speak Hebrew; among religious people, Hebrew was used for prayers and for religious studies, and women were exempt from religious studies. It is a holy language, they say, and must not be profaned by mundane conversations. My grandmother talked to me in Yiddish, and I struggled to answer her in kind.

At age six I often stand beside my father when he prays at home during the week. As required by Jewish law we face east, in the direction of the Old City where the Temple once stood. I have a towel over my shoulders, imitating him wearing a *talit*, and I rock back and forth, pretending to pray. I like the rocking, a plea to God. While pretending, the gesture is my own.

With the approach of Sukkot I like to watch my father build the Sukkah. His hands move steadily, hammering nails into the wooden boards. He climbs a ladder and puts branches on the top. I help him decorate the Sukkah, hanging bright-colored crepe in the shapes of fruit. In the Sukkah my father holds my hands as I hold the *lulav* and *ethrog*, the palm branch and citron. He directs them towards the east, south, west, north, and up and down, and I say the blessings with him. I feel proud and privileged to do what he does, to do what a man does. We continue to recite the Sukkot blessings through *Hoshana Rabbah*, the seventh day of Sukkot. On that day my father once again asks me to pray with him. He holds my hands as I hold a bundle of willow branches, and as I repeat the blessing after him we beat the bundle on a chair and recite three times, "The voice of the herald heralds and proclaims." This is a plea to God to save His nation. But what really matters is the pleasure I take in the power with which my father and I beat the bundle on the chair.

On the Sabbath, upon returning from the synagogue, we have lunch. My mother places a bottle of arrack (an alcoholic Mediterranean beverage) on the table with small glasses. Even when I am very young, before I become a teenager, my father pours two glasses of arrack—for him and me—as we eat gefilte fish, encouraging me to drink. It is good, he says, you will learn to like it. I like the cloudy near-mystical look of the arrack in the glass. And I drink it in one or two gulps, savoring my father's prodding and the sharp taste of the drink.

When night falls on Saturday, people look up to see if there are three stars in the sky: that means Sabbath is over. Sometimes I hear people argue about whether there are two stars or three. I wait excitedly for the uncertainty to be relieved. Marking the end of the Sabbath my father says the *Havdalah* prayer over a cup of wine. I feel proud my parents trust me to hold the lit, multi-stranded candle, careful to follow what they say: Hold it high so you will have a tall husband. A short while before the prayer there is already a flutter in the house, a slight commotion typical of weekdays. I wait for the moment when I can extinguish the flame in a bit of wine, the moment of separation between the holy and the common, of awe mingled with a sense of relief, a sudden change from a restful mood to an active one.

2

A MAN OF THE OLD CITY

During the War of Independence the Arabs captured the Old City of Jerusalem. My father dreams of praying there, at the Wailing Wall, and whenever he prays he imagines finding the perfect mossy crack in the wall, to stuff in his note to God. He claims his faith is not as deep as my mother's, that he has doubts. The Old City of Jerusalem is the birthplace of his faith, his wavering faith, and a lure for it. It is not clear to me whether my father's doubts are about the power of God or the efficacy of religious practice. More likely, his anxiety about some catastrophic future overrides his faith. He must fear that the future will be as bleak as it was in his childhood.

For nineteen years, from the Independence War in 1948 until the recapturing of the Old City in 1967, my father waited at the threshold of the Old City. For nineteen years he waited like the grasses on the third day of creation that, according to the Midrash (a tool to interpret Biblical texts), stayed at the portal of the earth until the sixth day of creation, when the first man sought compassion for them, whereupon the rains fell, and they grew.

After this long separation my father is eager to visit places that are a part of his past. He takes me to visit the Temple Mount. With my father, the Old City feels open and welcoming. I think of the time in the past when they used to close the gates of the city every night, and those who arrived late had to stay outside. Before we enter the Al-Aqsa Mosque, my father and I take off our shoes. My mother waits outside, adhering to the prohibition to enter non-Jewish places of worship. The interior walls, adorned by mosaics, emanate such venerable stillness that I become attuned to a silence that belongs to all religions at their highest.

My father also takes me along to visit the archaeological digs near the

Wailing Wall. I can see him standing there, exhilarated, intently watching the excavations, as if waiting for something to unfold. He wants to locate his father's gravesite, his father who collapsed and died on a street in Istanbul many years earlier. Until the end of his life my father tries to find out where the grave is, but his inquiries are in vain. He remembers his father's kind face and his small beard, and is certain that he will see him again at the resurrection of the dead. I will be old and gray, he would say, while my father will be younger, only thirty-six years old.

As we stroll, my father shows me the neighborhood where he lived as a child. He tells me that during the time the new city was separated from the old, he longed to visit the neighborhood he grew up in, to touch the tombs, now mostly destroyed by the Arabs, in which his ancestors were buried. He wanted to be nearer to their spirits.

We also visit the site of the first Ashkenazi synagogue, the Hurva. The Hurva once belonged to the Ashkenazi Jews; its unfinished structure was burned, together with forty Torahs, by Arab creditors. As a little girl, my father's great-great-grandmother Zelda was among those who volunteered to clear the site and help carry stones to rebuild the synagogue. A legendary figure in the Old City, Zelda was famous for her energy and piety, entertaining at weddings and praying the midnight lamentations over the destruction of the temple, prostrating on graves of *tzaddikim* (righteous men) in the cemetery on the Mount of Olives.

The Mount of Olives has an aura of holiness and also of impurity. Many tzaddikim are buried there. Among them is my mother's father, who moved to Jerusalem in the late twenties to be buried there, a custom that still prevails among religious Jews in Diaspora. A bit further away is Mount Zion. King David, according to some, is buried there; others deny it. As a child I didn't like visiting the tomb because of this uncertainty, and when I did, I kept thinking that maybe the place is a lie.

Zelda's enthusiasm over rebuilding the Hurva reminds me of the exiles returning from Babylon to Eretz Yisrael under the inspired leadership of Ezra the Scribe, to rebuild the second temple and to dedicate it to God. I admired Ezra, but it was Cyrus, King of Persia, who captured my imagination and became my true hero. He sent the Jews back to their land to worship in their temple. He was the most magnanimous of all rulers, understanding that people have a need for religion, any religion.

Zelda's father, the artist Mordecai Schnitzer, came to Eretz Yisrael from Poland in 1810. As a young man and student in the Beit Midrash, he had a dream about a holy ark with elaborate engravings. When he awoke he was inspired to buy artistic tools, and he started building the envisioned ark. He became a sculptor and a painter, a restorer and builder of holy arks, a man who lived inside his art. While living in Jerusalem he made objects of art for visiting British and Austro-Hungarian royalty. Among the stories about him was one about how he selected the stone for the cornerstone he was assigned to carve for the synagogue in Vienna: He hopped from rock to rock in the mountains surrounding the Old City; completely absorbed in his search, he tapped each rock until he found one whose sound he liked, and then he had it mined.

On another visit to the Old City, my father shows me off to his former Arab customers, who sit on low stools by their shops. He says in Arabic, Here is my daughter who was that little girl you knew before 1948. We enter a stationery shop. Pens lie on a counter beneath glass, and the smell of paper permeates the place. I recall my father's shop. My father and the owner of the shop are chatting amiably. It is as if time has risen above the long, inimical journey they both had been forced to take, and has stood still.

After the walk, my father and I stop by a small Arab coffee house. We sit outside. The sun is hot, but we sit at a table covered with a canopy. My father orders Turkish coffee. He lights a cigarette and sits back. His face is relaxed. Lines of sorrow and worry that usually inhabit his face are gone. He is back home.

In spite of having spirited ancestors such as Zelda and her father, I believed there was no real pedigree in my genealogy. My father would tell me that we are descendants of a great Hasidic rabbi, Reb Shmelke from Nikolsburg. It left no impression on me until years later when I read Martin Buber's book on Hasidism and was able to understand how greatness is akin to simplicity. I would have been excited if I'd had a tie to the great actors of our Hebrew theater, such as Hannah Rovina—her facial features were perfectly carved, her deep voice saturated with meaning, and when she played in "The Dybbuk," she transcended all limitations. Or Yigal Alon, a commander in the *Palmach*, the elite Jewish underground fighting force during the British Mandate, who symbolized a strong generation that exuded freedom and confidence. Or the poet Natan Alterman, who spoke of the national struggle for independence. Many of his poems were banned by the British authorities. Alterman was in a habit of sitting in Café Cassit in Tel Aviv and drinking coffee with his artist friends. What were they talking about? I was intrigued.

As a teenager I wanted my father to be different. I wanted him to dress better. His stained shirt and crumpled pants annoyed me. I complained about it to my mother, who said, This is the way Father is. Couldn't she do anything about it? I fantasized that my father was driving a car on our small and dusty street. It was not the car that interested me but my father driving it, which, in my eyes, transformed him from the small and anxious man he was into a brave and daring one. Where did the idea of my father driving a car come from? None of his friends drove. Not even Feldman, a childhood friend who moved from the Old City of Jerusalem to Petah Tikva. Feldman owned orchards, and my father had a picture of him on a horse by his orchard. Whenever he came to visit us he talked about his kidney stones and said he needed to drink eight cups of tea a day to dissolve them. He sat on our terrace and gulped down one cup of tea after another. I thought of him as a hero, and the non-stop drinking of tea added to my idea of him as a hero. I could see that my father admired him too. Maybe because he took unusual risks, like moving out of his childhood city and becoming a farmer. A farmer who became rich. At times my father talked about moving to a place in the country, having a small farm and a garden. My father wanted peace of mind. And he imagined that a farm would provide it.

My father does not follow this dream. But after he retires he studies Talmud every morning, something he aspired to do all his life. He adheres more rigorously to rituals. He rises with my mother at 5 a.m. and goes to the synagogue to pray. He devotes time to sending checks to the needy. He doesn't refuse people who ask him for money. My father's early responsibilities made him a very worried man, but it made him autonomous. He is decisive. His conflicts, if he has any, are not apparent. I can still see his quick, confident walk in the streets of the Old City, sharing with me his past, the neighborhood he grew up in, and his interest in all great places of worship.

My father is a man of habit. During his years working in the store he comes home every day at 1 p.m. for lunch. He looks weary. He declares impatiently that he is hungry. My mother serves him lunch quickly. Then he takes a nap. When he wakes up, though the lines on his face are a bit smoother, he still looks burdened. He must return to the store to reopen at 4 p.m. My father says, I am not as ambitious as some of my competitors, Feinstein and Cohen. People trust me, he continues, I have my customers, and it is sufficient. I have had a couple of offers for partnerships, but I like to be my own boss, not get involved with other people's ways of doing things. My mother nods. She agrees. Feinstein is very ill, my mother says, he has been too ambitious. My mother is protective of my father's health; she doesn't want him to work as hard as Feinstein and ruin his health.

The store in its heyday was a meeting place. My friends would stop there to buy supplies. My architect friend Reuven would linger in the store and chat with my parents after buying supplies. (At some point when I was growing up my mother started helping my father in the store.) My girlfriend Dina would occasionally stop by to borrow money. Juan, the Spanish consul to Jerusalem, whom I met on a boat coming back from New York, once stopped there and left me a note inviting me to a party. (He was unable to call me because we had no phone.) My father said, Such a nice guy, what a pity he is not Jewish.

My father says he hates the store. But he never says what he hates about it. And when I ask him what he would have liked to do instead, he says he would have liked to sing. I recall Ferrer, an old Cuban singer, who sings about love and longing. He sings about being hungry as a child. He sings about gardenias. There were no gardenias in the Old City of Jerusalem. But my father would have liked to sing.

When my older son was a child, my father would "employ" him as a cashier in his store. My son would stand by the cashier, a big smile on his face, giving change to customers. In my early twenties I would go to the store to ask for money to supplement my salary, and my father would take paper bills out of his cash register and ask, How much do you need? Before I had a chance to answer, he, with a twinkle in his eye, happy to be unstinting, flipped several bills and gave them to me and asked if I would like more. My mother would tell me that my father loved me more than anything else in the world. Whenever he saw me in a new dress, he would say it looked good on me. Sometimes when my mother and I tried on the same dress he would say it looked better on me. I felt guilty about this comment, but my mother did not seem to mind. It was clear to me that my father loved her too.

Throughout his life my father would talk about how emaciated I was after being sick with typhus for a month. I was *very* sick. He would talk about how small I became. I am three. I am sitting in the palm of his hand. He is standing on the terrace; he has taken me outside to be in the sun. Perhaps my father thought I would not survive. He thought he was losing me, the way he lost his father and his brothers, the way his family lost everything after his father died in Istanbul and was buried without a trace. He lost his childhood. I am skin and bones, but I've survived. He hasn't lost me. He talks with sadness and pride about the moment he took me outdoors. He talks about how he held me, like that, in the palm of his hand.

What is it you are playing? my father inquires. I say, Mozart, or Chopin, and he writes it on the inside of the bathroom medicine cabinet. A few days later he says, Play the Mozart, it is very beautiful. As I play the piano my father looks at me lovingly, grateful for the gift. I am grateful for his remarks, though they are scarce, and usually uttered in an off-handed way. My father plainly says what he feels. He is not inclined to encourage me. He is mostly busy with his store and his customers. My father and I could have shared more. But his anger often gets in the way. And I am proud and un-appeasing. Now, I conjure up his kind face, the concern it expressed as he leaned to look at my leg after I underwent minor surgery, or the quiet, anxious way he recited the Psalms when I went to the emergency room because of stomach cramps.

My father says, You have a good head, you could be a lawyer. I wonder: Does he miss having a son? He says, I've donated money to the orphanage I was in, and they will see to it that someone says kaddish for me after I die. (It is not customary for a daughter to say kaddish for her parents.) My father is meticulously organized. He buys graves for himself and my mother, and every time he makes the slightest change in his will he shows it to me.

In 1988 my father calls me in New York. Without a warning he starts to sing. And he sings *Yah Ribbon Alam Vealmaya,* a sacred song in Aramaic sung after the Sabbath's midday meal. The song beckons God to return to his Temple and the Holy of Holies in Jerusalem, where every soul will be delighted. So sings my father in his small, warm, melodic voice: my father, who likes to listen to sacred music, is a cantor now; he sings to me, sings on the phone.

3

MY MOTHER'S LONGING

In 1931, when my mother is twenty-one years old, she leaves America and follows her father to Jerusalem to live with him and his wife. During the cold winter nights her father comes into her room and covers her; he calls her by her endearing middle name, Haikaleh, and my mother savors his touch, the fatherly touch she missed when she was a very young girl in a small town in Poland.

My mother is one of thousands of Jews who immigrated to Mandatory Palestine before World War II, not for Zionist or religious reasons, but because of the longing she had for her father who had immigrated several years before. During the two years she lived with her father and his third wife, my mother dressed modestly; she could only meet men arranged by a matchmaker. Her father was very strict, but my mother would speak about him with affection. I didn't mind following his rules, she would say, I loved him, and I loved those times when he cared for me tenderly.

After my mother married my father in 1933, she strayed from some of her father's fixed religious ways. She didn't cover her hair, and she wore short sleeves. On their honeymoon, my parents, along with some friends, hired donkeys and rode to the tomb of Rachel. My mother kept it a secret from her father, who would not have approved of such an adventurous excursion. When visiting him afterwards he wondered why she sat on the edge of a chair; she hid the fact that her rear was bruised from riding the donkey.

Even as a new bride, my mother would bring lunch to my father at his workplace. Every day she would walk there, from the north of the city east to the Old City. She walked with sure strides through the ancient gate of the walled city, which was still unfamiliar to her. Newness did not daunt her; she had the hope, or more likely the faith, that the days of want were over.

To their friends, my parents seemed an unlikely couple. My father's friends told him not to marry my mother: She is an American, she will demand a lot of money from you. My mother's friends also undermined her choice. He is too short, they said, he is not impressive. My mother notes that these friends remained unmarried; she prides herself for her ability to compromise.

My mother dislikes waste and scorns losing things. One day I came home from school without the lira she gave me. Determined to teach me a lesson she sent me back to school, a long way, to find it. She said, This is good upbringing. Her face was stern. Though my mother believes in moderation, she can be austere, like the city.

The different faces of my mother make me either fearful or happy. After my tonsils are taken out and I am still under the effect of ether and not sure where I am—the brownish-orange tiles in the hospital room look bumpy and unusually big as I look down from the crib I am lying in— my mother walks in with ice cream. Her smile is anxious and forced, and she does not ease my discomfort. I eat a bit of the ice cream, which hurts my throat, and to my mother's disappointment I refuse to eat more.

In a nightmare I frequently have, a face, I assume my mother's, travels towards me at an alarming speed, becoming bigger and bigger while losing its distinct features, like the bat that once flew by our terrace so close I feared it would get entangled in my hair or throw me into a panic if it brushed against me.

But on rainy days when I come home from school, wet to the bone, my mother's face emanates care. She takes off my boots, dries my feet, and sits me in front of the kerosene stove that warms only a small area. I stretch my arms above it, rubbing and warming my hands, while my mother prepares my favorite dish, a potato baked in a pot.

There are times when I am put to bed before dark and I look out at the bluish-white sky, hearing the children play outside, and wonder about my fate, this early bedtime. The image of my mother's face is that of indifference, busy in the kitchen or talking to a neighbor. When I am older, playing hide-and-seek behind a gate or a rock in the field, darkness descends on our neighborhood. As the neighborhood comes together in the dark, the houses look inward to their dim-lit interiors; as the darkness lasts and the hiding goes on, I imagine my mother waiting, impatiently.

There are only a few trees in our neighborhood. From my window I see a lone cypress tree as ancient as the city. During the day it is dusty and sad, but at night, under the stars, it stands erect. I like to look at that tree before going to bed when it meets the moon and the sky and the dark houses around it. On the Sabbath when I crawl into bed with my mother, she says, Look at the tree, that green, look at the sky, the birds, the world is beautiful, she says, the stars, the sea. And occasionally when she looks out of the window and sees a bird she says, I'd like to be a bird, and I wonder, why would she want to be a bird, doesn't she like being conscious of having a life?

The more affluent neighborhood, Rehavia, in the south of Jerusalem, has more trees. A dressmaker who makes pretty dresses for me lives there. In the spring my mother takes me to her house. We walk by gardens with sprinklers. The earth is wet, and there are many succulent plants. It is important that *you* choose the design, my mother says to me. I feel proud flipping through magazines and picking out the dresses I like.

My mother is often busy with washing my hair. She cuts it, washes it with egg yolk to give it an extra shine, and braids it. One day I am sent home from school because of lice in my hair. My mother instantly goes to work. She takes out the white basin from under a box-like bench that stands on the terrace, puts it on the stool in the bathroom, and places a can of kerosene next to it. She boils water and lets it cool a bit. Then she pours the water into the basin. I undress to the waistline, and as I bend over the basin, my mother rubs my hair and scalp with water and kerosene. She is indefatigable. She continues with the process for a number of days until we get rid of the lice.

At times when I am ill, I ask my mother to sit next to me on my bed.

Sometimes she is busy in the kitchen and I call her several times before she comes. As soon as she comes and sits next to me and I feel the touch of her body and see the sympathetic look on her face, I feel soothed and my discomfort leaves me. Once I had sharp stomach cramps at night, and since we didn't have a phone, my mother ran to the doctor. At three o'clock in the morning she ran to fetch him, and he came and gave me an injection. My mother took me to her bed and put her arm around me and I fell asleep, her arm barring any more pain that might come my way.

When I am eleven I tell my parents I no longer want to go with them to the Horowitzes' on Friday night. I don't know why I am suddenly unwilling: where do I get the courage to take a stand on something that seems important to them? My parents say nothing. I have been granted the freedom to say no, to do as I wish. Though my mother is exacting, though she is strict, I know that I can get her to change her mind. I feel blessed when my mother says, Okay, you will have a piano and you will have piano lessons, or she says, I want you to choose your own dress, and above all, when she says, Okay, you can go to summer camp, after I plead and weep and fast. After I stay in my parents' bedroom and for a long time I do not come out, my mother finally acquiesces and says those memorable words that set me free, Okay, you can go.

When I am in my teens, my mother accompanies my father once a month on business trips to Tel Aviv. I know she goes away untroubled. She trusts me to be alone. On these days, I eat lunch at a restaurant, ordering food I like, wieners and mashed potatoes. I feel free and independent, especially when the waiter asks me for my order, and later when I pay. After lunch I climb the street that leads to my house. It is early afternoon; the streets are empty and the stores closed. There is loneliness, marked by a quiet satisfaction that there is care, and that the day marches on, with only a pleasant break in continuity.

The excursions with my mother are of a different nature than those I have with my father. Having emigrated from New York, my mother has a taste for movies and the theater. There are a number of movie houses in Jerusalem, with names like Eden or Rex or Studio, that show Hollywood movies. My mother takes me along with her to see movies such as *The Snake Pit, Bambi*, or *Dr. Jekyll and Mr. Hyde*. She picks me up on Saturday nights to go to the movies while I am involved in activities organized by Bnei-Akiva, the youth wing of the national religious movement. I resent my mother picking me up to go to the movies, but I'm only nine or ten and it feels futile to voice my objection. These movies, however, make a dent, and later on I'm glad I saw them. Their drama and imagination give me a taste of a world elsewhere, beyond my routine life and the confines of the city. My mother would talk to me about her favorite actors, Leslie Howard and Frederic March. She tells me about the death of Howard in a plane crash. He was young, refined looking, and such a good actor, she says. And Frederic March, a woman's dream, handsome and a gentleman. When a classmate of mine tells me that her brother is the actor Robert Taylor, I am very excited and tell it to my mother, who says it isn't true. I am very angry with my mother for not believing it.

On rare occasions my mother takes me to see a play put on by a theater in Tel Aviv, where all the theater companies are. The companies have names like *Hamatateh* (The Broom) and *Ohel* (Tent). Once, she takes me to see a play in Yiddish; my father comes along. It is an unusual treat to be awake late at night, sitting on my mother's lap and watching a play far away from Jerusalem.

My mother is angry with me whenever I don't do what she wants me to do, but she is never angry when members of her family visit from New York. Every summer, one of my mother's brothers and his wife, or one of her nieces or nephews, come to Jerusalem, and there is a commotion, the air full of excitement and adulation. My parents go to the airport to welcome them, waiting in the heat of summer.

My cousin Benjamin remembers my parents waiting for him at the airport with fresh plums to give him as soon as he lands. The family visits us in our home, and the conversation is mostly in English, sometimes in Yiddish for my father's sake (my father knows very little English). I know every member of my mother's family from the stories my mother tells me about them. Though the stories are real—they involve what is good *and* bad about her family—the tone of my mother's voice is tinged with idealization. Her favorite brother is the one nicknamed "Roite"—for his red hair. He is rich. His wife, very generous with her gifts, brings me clothes, which I sometimes give to my friends—there are so many of them. The gifts include costume jewelry, a piano, and a refrigerator. My parents pride themselves in never asking for any of that, and never asking for financial help. I realize later that this connection with my family has prepared me for my life in New York.

My mother works hard to please her family, making elaborate meals for them. While she is focused on them, she pays less attention to me. They can drive to our house on the Sabbath; she does not object. I enjoy the lack of her overbearing attention, but as soon as her family leaves, she returns to being intolerant. She finds fault with the chores I perform; she undermines my ability to do the simplest thing, such as peeling potatoes or cucumbers. You take off too much peel, she would say with extreme displeasure. And she blames me for my friends' shortcomings. If a friend misbehaves, does not return something she has borrowed, or breaks something in the house, my mother is quietly enraged. Later, this pattern of blaming continues. My mother quizzes me about a cousin who became nonreligious, making me, in some strange way, responsible for it. She is also critical of a Jewish girlfriend in New York who marries in a civil marriage. Why didn't she have a rabbi marry her? she asks in an accusatory voice. I feel threatened. I cannot stand up to my mother and declare my innocence. I don't even know that I am innocent. I think I am responsible for all the bad things these people do: why else would she ask me for their reason? I become defensive on their behalf. I try to explain why they did what they did. Sometimes I just want to flee.

My mother used to say that I don't know how fortunate I am to have a mother. She had lost her mother when she was a young girl in a small resort town in Galicia, a town bordered by forests and fields where she roamed barefoot picking strawberries. She would come home and often find her mother had gone off to another town seeking medical treatment for her crippled leg, a condition she was ashamed of. My mother's father and two of her oldest brothers had left Poland for America. They were not able to bring the rest of the family to join them because World War I had begun. My mother was often hungry. She shared her hunger with her brother, and she would struggle with having to wait for her mother to come back, making the best of it, as she would often say. Once when she and her mother visited rich relatives, a wonderful smell of pancakes came from the kitchen. When asked whether she wanted pancakes, she said no. She was hungry, but proud. After the war my mother's mother feared going to the States with a diseased leg, but although reluctant, she was willing. Then, three days before she and her two children — my nine-year-old mother and her eleven-year-old brother — were to board a ship that would take them to the States to reunite with her husband and her older sons, she became ill with dysentery and died.

I can see my mother, a little girl on a boat going to America, accompanied by a stranger, a German woman assigned by my mother's relatives to look after the children on the boat; a little girl whose mother had suddenly died; a little girl with red hair and freckles, standing on the deck of a ship, with no one to wave to, abandoned to the care of a stranger. She could still see her mother's face paling, thinned by a sudden disease. And there is my mother, a little girl whose time is eternal, who longs for the father she barely knows, weeping for days after her mother's death, the mother she loved, the mother who had taken her to her bed at night. There is the little girl on a ship, a white ribbon in her red hair, she looks at the sea and feels distances: everything good and nourishing is at a distance, but she never stops hoping. Standing on the ship's deck she weeps and continues to hope. The billowing sea doesn't frighten her; even the night, the night on the deck, and all that darkness does not frighten her. She sees the sea and imagines meeting her father. She sees the stars and imagines meeting her father.

When my mother arrived at the pier in New York she jumped on the first man with a beard she saw, thinking it was her father. For a moment she is hanging on to this man, this stranger, but it doesn't take long, another moment perhaps, and her excitement becomes as hollow as an image of the violin her mother had promised her once they were in America. She was thrilled to finally meet her father, but soon learned he couldn't look after her because he had to go to work.

At first my mother, along with her youngest brother, lived in Jewish

Harlem. She remembers it fondly as a lively, busy neighborhood with many Jewish stores. Occasionally she was moved from one brother to another. When her father remarried she went to live with him. She came home one day to find the apartment empty; her father's new wife had left, taking all the furniture.

My mother's family entrusted her to her oldest brother's care. He was married and had several children. Her brother paid little attention to her or to his family. His wife was depressed. My mother tells me how Sylvia, her sister-in-law, spoiled the children, wouldn't let them do any chores in the house. My mother, a child herself at the time, helped raise the children and did most of the housework. She was a servant. But she does not complain about it; my mother rarely complains. When I was growing up she was seldom sick, and when she was, she lay in bed, quiet, calm; I remember her lying on her back, I remember her eyes, thoughtful in a dreamy sort of way, she would lie in her bed wrapped in her own world, her blanket encased in a white starched duvet, looking out of the window, and when I would ask her if she needed anything, she would ask for a glass of water and something to eat that hardly required preparation.

As my mother ages, and her mind weakens, and her defenses crumble, I am able to read into the silence of her youth. I see her as having a keen intelligence: everyone in her family sees she is brilliant, everyone in her family knows she could make something out of herself, but they are silent about it. They ignore her brilliance; it doesn't exist. When she is sick with pneumonia her brother takes her to his younger brother's house. She has no one on her side, no one to turn to for support. She is an orphan. Her family tosses her around. She is at her younger brother's home, isolated, in a separate room, coughing, with pneumonia. She hears her family talking in the other room, but she is not allowed to go there because of her germs. She does not ask for and does not demand anything; she knows not to ask for anything, not to want anything that is not handed to her. Since her mother's death she has kept her unhappiness to herself. She is grateful for the hot milk they keep bringing her, and she tells me how well she is taken care of. She is grateful to her family in New York, who provided her with a home, and is sympathetic to Sylvia, her sister-in-law, though she was over-demanding. To soften what must have been humiliating experiences, she says, Sylvia treated me as a helpmate in the household, but also as her companion; we would go the movies together. We would have interesting conversations. Sylvia was brilliant, but she couldn't cope with the demands her life and her family made on her.

At her older brother's house my mother becomes a voracious reader. She locks herself in the bathroom to read. It is her escape, her respite. My mother knows her family is not giving her the opportunity to which she is entitled: to attend high-school, to receive a higher education. And she is discontented. Later, my mother talks to me about the books she reads. She likes biographies. She tells me about George Bernard Shaw's interest in bodily health. She likes to read about energetic, active women who are independent thinkers, such as Eleanor Roosevelt. I think she vaguely imagines herself being like these women.

My mother admires my pediatrician, Dr. Helena Kagan, a legendary figure who worked indefatigably for her patients, Jews and Arabs alike. Very early on my mother is aware of her greatness and may have felt a kinship with her. Perhaps she knows, unconsciously, that she, too, could have excelled professionally, if only she had received the education and the necessary backing.

Dr. Kagan is stern and has a wry smile; her no-nonsense presence, along with her imposing house, inspires confidence. My mother enjoys telling and retelling how often Dr. Kagan saved her and me from unnecessary painful treatments by exercising good judgment. Once, when I am a year old, a cousin visiting from America gives me a small box of aspirins to play with. Suddenly my mother notices that the box is open and the aspirin gone; she runs sobbing to Dr. Kagan, who says, I am convinced that your daughter didn't swallow the aspirins, she is an intelligent girl, and would not keep anything in her mouth that tastes bad. The doctor sends us home without pumping my stomach. My mother never doubts Dr. Kagan's common sense. When at three I become ill with typhus, Dr. Kagan makes a house visit. She reassures my mother that I would get better treatment at home than in the hospital. You keep the house so clean, and you take good care of your child, she says to my mother;

a hospital would not be nearly as good. Her confidence in herself is infectious. My mother keeps me at home, and I recover after a month.

My mother reveres doctors. Dr. Ticho, the renowned eye doctor, practices in a quaint thick-walled house that later becomes a showcase for his wife's artwork. Once, when a tiny white ball develops in the interior part of my eyelid, my mother takes me to him and he compliments her for bringing me in early, before the ball had developed into something "unpleasant." It is not clear what that unpleasantness would have been, but whenever my mother talks about Dr. Ticho, she is grateful that such a venerable doctor approved of her action, and that she had saved the two of us from a mysterious, unpleasant experience.

It is 1966 and I am on a summer visit in Jerusalem. I leave my boys with my mother and am strolling in the streets of Rehavia, in south Jerusalem. It is 2 p.m. I protect myself from the scorching sun by walking under trees that line the sidewalk. The streets are empty; it is siesta time. I like the emptiness, the stillness, the way the street abandons itself to the fierce light of the sun. I roam alone as if called to observe this numbing void and fulfill some mysterious task. It is here, in this low and sprawling modern building that I now face, that I attended music classes. Here that I often felt my body was drained of vitality, my mind dazed. I feel like a murderer who returns to the scene of her crime where something terrible and unacceptable has been committed: my failure to succeed.

Back home my mother looks at me, as she often does, with such longing, as if I wasn't there. She wants to be close to me—though she never says so explicitly. She waits impatiently for my letters when I am in New York. I have always been struck by the intensity of her longing. It resembles my father's longing for his father. It is a longing that never leaves her; it is her most pronounced characteristic. For days she cried for her mother, and for her father whom she last saw when she was two years old, until she met him again in New York after World War I. I remember her standing on the pier in Haifa, when my husband and I left on a ship sailing to France and then to America on our way to New York. Her eyes rose to the deck where I stood. She was on the pier with my father, waving to me, her right arm raised halfway up. I recalled her waving to me, a well-wishing kind of waving, when I had left for the army. But now she lifts her arm hesitantly, reluctantly, as if she were in pain. She is already longing for me, her only child, longing for everyone in her life who abandoned her; longing for her mother.

4

A DOMESTIC LIFE

After I leave Israel, in 1962, my mother, substitutes for my absence by adding new restrictions to her religious rituals. Her new neighborhood, her new community, more religious than her previous one had been, influences her. It has its eyes on her, as it does on everyone else. Judaism is the best religion, she says, and indicates that any Jew who thinks differently is a heretic. The *goyim* are out to harm us, she adds, and the practice of Judaism is what saves us. All Jews must live in Israel. Being a convert to her own homeland makes her adamant. My mother doesn't cling to material things, but she clings to her ideologies. I am terrified to disagree with her; I think I might hurt her feelings or offend her community. I hear my thoughts spinning but I don't have the words to express them. Perhaps her community puts a damper on my thoughts, making them blurry. My thoughts seem to solidify in the recesses of the mind, and somewhere in the dark they become an emotion, a regret, an anger.

My mother attends synagogue more regularly than before. She also takes classes in religion. She covers her hair, and will not go to the movies. She throws herself into performing acts of charity, visiting the sick and the needy. She gains the trust of a schizophrenic woman and of a depressed neighbor, and she persists in caring for them. Her faith strengthens. We must continue, she says; the way to live better is by helping others, she adds. She is steadfast in her belief that each one of us has a soul, a sacred core that ought to be respected, never violated. At the age of seventy, she gets up for anyone on the bus who seems old or fragile. And later, living in an old age home after suffering mini-strokes and loss of memory and the ability to function on her own, she is still able to help out a woman in a room across from hers who has lost the ability to walk to the dining room and to go to the bathroom on her own.

My mother welcomed anybody who came to our house and needed

help. The white-bearded man who collected *tzddakah* for poor people was invited for scrambled eggs, bread, and coffee; Ammar, the Arab man who cleaned our house, was invited to have coffee and cake after his work was done. It was irrelevant to my mother whether the beggars were in fact poor—those who came to her house or the ones sitting on the sidewalk next to the hospital Bikkur Cholim whom we passed on our way to visit my father's store. My mother would divide her change among the beggars with the utmost attention. The neighbor who fell into depression and unburdened herself by talking to my mother was encouraged by her to take walks in the market, where, in my mother's opinion, she would renew herself by looking at the fresh vegetables and fruits. One of my mother's relatives, recently divorced and in distress, stayed with my parents for a month and felt cured when she left. My mother did not point a finger at her, did not accuse her or her former husband or anyone else for the breakup. She and my father were simply present, supportive, and kind. Razali, our cleaning woman, was praised by my mother for her honesty. Razali was heavy and slow and it didn't matter to my mother whether she did a good job or not. Being accepting and hospitable was my mother's vicarious way of making up for losing her mother and her home at an early age, and for having to depend on others to raise her. Whoever comes to my home, she would say, I will make them feel wanted; I will never turn anyone away.

On my summer visits I watch with admiration as my mother rises at 5 a.m., washes her hands ritually, and without fail says the morning prayers and the afternoon prayers and recites the Psalms. She concentrates; she utters the words sincerely. My mother had always been indifferent to money and prestige. All she wanted in terms of money, she would say, is to be able to put her hand in her pocket and find there was the money she needed. In her new environment, she has become more vocal, more demonstrative about her thirst for knowledge and her interest in values and character. She expresses admiration for the modesty of my friend Avner, the well-known poet and a professor at the Hebrew University, who by all accounts should be proud. She backs up her beliefs with biblical references. The women she studies with commend her on her understanding and refer to her as the diamond in the crown.

My mother says, People say I could be a professional; I would make a good social worker. Perhaps she doubts this—why else would she refer to the opinion of others? Perhaps it is painful for her to acknowledge a desire she had not fulfilled. Perhaps she regrets not becoming a professional, but the regret came too late for her to do anything about it. Once, as a teenager, while staying at a younger brother's house, she was enrolled in a trade school to learn secretarial work. But she couldn't pursue it. She was soon called back by her older brother who said his family needed her. My mother talks very little about that part of her life. When she does she speaks with resignation, but without bitterness.

My mother feared that my being an intellectual would take me away from her, interfere with my emotional life, unbalance me. I thought I would feel lonely if I were distant from the warmth of her breath, the sound of her voice. During my years in school she discouraged me from doing my best: You'll never be a professor, she said. Why study so hard? She wanted to protect me from being frustrated, from being hurt, from disappointments. She would tell me about a nephew of hers who went to Harvard and had a nervous breakdown. But once, flying back to New York from a summer visit in Jerusalem, reading a poem by Uri Tzvi Greenberg, I started writing spontaneously and discovered that what I had written was a short poem about my younger son, his blue eyes, his sandals, his collection of blue stones. The visit in Jerusalem had been painful, sparked by arguments with my parents, and by an unprecedented occurrence: I had confronted my mother face to face, expressing my grievances about her expectations of me and the pressure she put on me to be observant, to be in constant touch with her, while denying my capabilities. The confrontation unblocked me, freed me to begin writing poetry.

I read one of my poems to my mother; she is silent. She looks away from me. When I speak about the seminar I teach, she talks about something else. Her expression hardens. My mother denies my talents by ignoring them. It is as if a revolution passes by her window and she doesn't see it. When I practice the piano, she never comments on my playing. Never. I can still sense her indifference, see the flow of her dress as she passes by me at the piano, from her bedroom to the corridor on her way to the kitchen and back. When my parents' friends visit, she asks me to play for them. As soon as I start to play, she and her friends begin to talk.

On a still afternoon at siesta time, on one of my visits to Jerusalem, as my father is taking his regular nap and the children are quietly playing, my mother and I discuss a newspaper article about an Israeli who translates English novels into Hebrew. The translator is a recluse, with a depressed outlook on the world. I too have been translating—Hebrew poetry into English and English poetry into Hebrew. My mother says, I hope you will not become like this man; whatever you do, you should do in moderation. My mother has not let go of her apprehension. I can see the muscles on her face tighten. She is worried that the long hours of translating will turn me into a hermit. I am dumbfounded, but I say nothing. Why would she think the man inspires me, or that I will fall into imitating him? Therein is a pattern of communication between my mother and myself. Often she says something that surprises me or hurts me, and I say nothing in return.

I am used to taking care of other people, family members, my mother would say. It seems inevitable to her. Her fate. She had cared for my two aunts, who relied on her for any social life they had. After they had died my grandmother came to live with us. Once again my mother was forced to compromise herself. She was under the prying eyes of my grandmother, who faulted her for everything, from her cooking to her clothes. When you were little, she says, my nephew from New York stayed with us for three years. He came to study at a yeshiva, and he constantly criticized your father for what in his eyes was laxity in the practice of religious rituals. Three years. And now your grandmother does the same to me. I feel angry with my grandmother. I want to protect my mother from her criticism, from all unhappiness. I understand my mother wanting to be a bird, to fly, to flee.

After my grandmother dies, my parents feel free to travel. My husband and I, along with our boys, begin to take my parents on trips. Once we take them to the hotel in Tiberius where Mark and I had our honeymoon. When my mother opens the door that leads to the terrace of her room and sees Lake Kinneret at the foot of the building, tranquil and expansive, glittering in the afternoon sun, she becomes transfixed. She runs towards me, she looks younger than her years, she has a little girl's smile on her face and her eyes shine, and she embraces me tightly.

After my mother loses my father and before she has a stroke, there is a change in her. She expresses an interest in what I am doing, in my writing, and even in my seminar work, which promotes the value of studying the great religions. As her mind begins to deteriorate she is still able to keep up her interest. I call her twice a week from New York and tell her about my week's events. I tell her about difficulties I experience in giving a seminar that has to do with a rare student being disruptive, or about my demanding work in hospice as a social worker, or about the hurdles in my writing. She says, Life is not a bowl of cherries, or, Your work in hospice is a mitzvah, or, Keep writing: the more you write the more you'll like it and the better you'll be at it. It is a relief to hear she relates to me not as a child that needs protection, a child of whom she approves or disapproves, but as an adult who is her equal, with whom she can share her views.

2000, Jerusalem. My mother's body and mind are weak. She has become very forgetful. When she wakes up from an afternoon nap she may think it is nighttime. Her confusion draws me close to her. Her demands of me are fading out, just like her sky-blue eyes, which sometimes close involuntarily. My mother endures, bears up. Her quietude is like nature: organic, whole. When ill she lies still in bed, the skin of her face smooth, her expression dreamy. I wonder about how quiet she is, how perfectly calm.

When I am in New York, my older son and his wife look after her, devotedly. They are like an anchor. Ari, my friend who unreservedly and without fail gives a helping hand when needed, visits her regularly. Once when she was ill, and I was teaching a seminar, he said, You don't have to come, I will care for her. Ari, who was born in Europe, adds old world spice to my mother's life. He brings her flowers. He embraces her. He calls her *maidaleh* (a young girl in Yiddish).

Only a few years ago, when my husband and I planned to take our grandchildren for a hike on the outskirts of Jerusalem, my mother asked to join us. We thought because of her age and the weakness she often experienced, it was not a good idea. Mostly, we thought, her slow pace would interfere with ours, and we would have to look after her, and wouldn't be able to focus on our grandchildren. My mother persisted; she begged to join us. I can make it, she pleaded, I spend most days alone in the house, and I'd like to go. It will be too strenuous for you, we pleaded in return. I can still see the expression of disappointment on her face, and something in me collapses. Why wasn't I more generous?

My husband and I take my mother to a restaurant. She talks very little; mostly she seems to be living inside her slow-moving mind. She says, Everything passes, everything passes. She is consoled by impermanence. She longs for my father. She remembers joking with him about who would die first. She feels my father has won the contest; by dying first, he has won. Not even I, her only child, can make up for his absence.

Every day my mother continues to say the morning prayers and the afternoon prayers and recites the Psalms of the day. Though her mind has weakened, she says them with fervor. When I am tired, I lie next to her in her bed and hold her hand, and it is as comforting to me as it is to her. My mother and I have come to the present, as Rilke did, unfinished. We reproach ourselves. We agonize over minute things. But I remember some complete days. Waiting to see three stars that signal the end of the Sabbath, I would sit on my mother's lap on the terrace while she sang "Gott Fun Avrohom" to me, the Yiddish prayer for the week recited only by women. And then she would lose her concreteness; her voice, soft and nostalgic, spoke and sang, recitative style.

How agile my mother was, squatting to light the primus, as we called it, a kerosene-fueled, one-burner stove, in order to fry schnitzel or heat the laundry pot. With what speed she would bake a cake (my father and I careful not to slam doors lest the cake collapse), how effortless the movements of her hands when she made lunch, the big meal of the day: eggplant in tomato sauce on Mondays, boiled cow's brain on Tuesdays, on Wednesdays fried fish, and on Thursdays cauliflower in tomato sauce.

Friday nights, the beginning of the Sabbath, we had gefilte fish, chicken soup, chicken, and salad, and for dessert, compote. On the Sabbath my mother served my favorite dish: *cholent* (a kind of stew that simmers overnight). I ate whatever was served to me, even the compote, which I did not like.

My mother was a consummate shopper. She would say, The fish and vegetables I buy have to be fresh. I remember standing with her in the fish store on Geulah Street, in front of a tank filled with carp. The fish looked identical to me, but my mother, with determination and expertise, found one fish best to her liking. At home she filled the bathtub with water and put the fish in it. When she was ready to cook, she placed the fish on a newspaper on the marble shelf in the kitchen and killed it with one or two blows of an ax. Once when I was home alone, a fish my mother had put in the bathtub jumped out, gasping and wriggling on the floor. I was afraid to touch it, and I ran to my friend Rina who lived a block away. She came back with me and fearlessly put the fish back in the bathtub.

On days my mother didn't go to the big market on Mahane Yehuda, she shopped in the neighborhood vegetable store, which was also on Geulah Street. She inquired about how fresh the vegetables were, when they had arrived, why some didn't look fresh, or why the selection was poor. The owner, who looked grim and worn out, answered her every question. I saw he liked her.

Having been restricted to a domestic life is what my mother knows. It is a form of life she passed on to me, replete with familial and social possibilities and the pleasures of friendships, but without professional ones. Though her short-term memory is gone, she still retains a capacity to think and to feel. My mother lacks a formal education, but she is a quick thinker and has a wide range of feelings. Knowing that she won't remember what I tell her, I feel free to talk about what saddens me. She responds with care. When I tell her about a fight Mark and I had, she makes a distinction between a fight and an argument. When you fight, she says, you don't think; when you argue you think and you attempt to reach an agreement. My mother mostly enjoys me telling her about her childhood. She listens intently as I tell her that after her father had left for

America, she shared her mother's bed, a comfort to them both. And she smiles widely as I remind her that she enjoyed roaming barefoot in her beloved forest, picking strawberries. Each time I visit her, she says, You are a good daughter.

5

WITHOUT A RIVER OR SEA

Everyone knows that to live in Jerusalem one must suffer discomfort. It is a city without a river or sea and it rations its electricity and water. The electricity in Jerusalem sometimes fails. When this happens everyone goes out on their terraces. One can hear people shouting to each other making sure the failure is not theirs alone. When this is confirmed, everyone goes inside to light kerosene lamps. No one complains. Inside, I watch the flame in the glass while the house fills with adventure. My mother is especially calm in these moments.

Water supplies are also limited. Some of the city's courtyards have cisterns. Our neighbors on the ground floor are lucky to have one. The sound of their pump is the sound of life, loud and energetic. The water, fresh and cold, comes out in splashes. My mother heats the water by burning wood. During my once-a-week shower, my father keeps knocking on the door for me to hurry. The water from the showerhead is usually sparse and I linger there, testing my father's patience.

Yet to be born and raised in Jerusalem gives one a special status. People in other countries long to live here. Perhaps it is the clear air that arouses longing, or the sky like a blue dome. Perhaps it is the Wailing Wall—a remnant of the Temple in the Old City, or the ancient tombstones of tzaddikim. Whenever I say that I am from Jerusalem the response is, O! Jerusalem! Asked to elaborate, people say that it is a special city, majestic, spiritual.

At night Jerusalem is very quiet. The cafés and shops are closed, and nightlife is restricted to a couple of bars where foreigners and single people seek companionship.

People rave about the beauty of the city's surrounding mountains. But

in town the streets are narrow, houses crammed, dust rises, and everywhere the color gray. Beggars sit on a hilly road across from a hospital.
A lone policeman directs traffic where the two main streets meet at the
center. The kiosk on the corner sells soda mixed with raspberry syrup.

There are very few dogs in our city. Our street has a German Shepherd
that belongs to a German-Jewish couple. I think that dog has never seen
another dog. His face is sad as he looks through the rails of his terrace.
Does he wonder about his strange fate? Whenever he is let loose, which
is seldom, he chases birds and cats, causing consternation among the
neighbors. The alley cats are sometimes in heat all at once, crying and
growling all night long. It is difficult to ignore them; they suffer so — their
yearnings unrequited. They possess our street and our souls.

Jerusalem is steeped in Judaism, as well as Islam and Christianity. I don't
think about these other religions, and I don't think about the city's great
historical moments like the Crusades. I know nothing about the Russian
Orthodox religion, whose compound is in the center of town in a huge,
open space. When I walk by in summer I can only think of the scorching
sun beating down on the compound with a blinding light. Every day,
on my way to school, I pass by an abandoned minaret that stands in the
middle of a bare, thorny field. Yet I am neither curious about nor interested in Islamic worship.

Summers and winters in Jerusalem are harsh. On summer days when a
sirocco settles in and the city is laden with heat, I like to curl up on the
couch and read translated novels like *Germinal* and *The Forsyte Saga*. The
city slips away while I picture a couple in a French village making love
in a coal mine, or a couple in an elegant carriage galloping through the
streets of London. I don't understand *Jean-Christophe*, but I read it with
fascination.

My parents and I go to the Savoy Hotel on the beach in Tel Aviv for a
week. Just as we do every year we get burnt by the sun — we develop
large blisters and our skins peel for weeks. The vacation is dull, except
for meeting Australian soldiers who serve in the British Mandate and
who also vacation in the hotel. They cheer things up, joyfully chatting

with my mother. They wear wide-brimmed hats, shorts with knee-high socks, and they are very loud. I think they look silly. My friends seem to have more exciting vacations. One travels by train, with her parents and sisters, to her family in Cairo. I imagine they must be doing exotic things though I don't know what they are. Another visits her aunt at a kibbutz. The kibbutz is left-wing, and I imagine the members are strong, and tan, and fearless, unlike us Jerusalemites who are un-tanned, and considered by the rest of the country to be studious, indoor types.

After summer, a long, dry season, the arrival of the first rain is an event. I love the first rain—sparse, restrained, with drops as big as marbles—and the iridescence after. Streets soften, gloomy buildings open up, rejoicing in the rain's blessings. At night, as I lie in bed listening to the rain, I am closer to myself, as if a kiss or a holy message penetrates me.

In winter we huddle around a kerosene stove that stands in the middle of the living room. It takes the edge off the cold, but fails to keep us warm. My father tends the stove, filling it up with kerosene when needed. Coming home after getting wet in the rain, we put our clothes on two chairs next to the stove.

When it snows, which is rare, the city is silent and remote. The buses stop running; there are no other means of transportation. The snow covers the familiar field and the grapevine I like to look at. I wait for the sun or rain to end this white loneliness so that I can go out and play.

Once, on a snowy Sabbath day, when I am six, the blue blanket with which my mother covers the tin unit that houses the kerosene cooking stove (on which the cholent has been simmering) catches on fire. The apartment is filled with smoke. I am carried to our Sephardic neighbors next door. We have no phone, and it is too far to walk over to the firehouse. The father in the Sephardic family, a handyman at a hospital, fearlessly steps into the kitchen and extinguishes the fire. Meanwhile, I have a good time with his children, jumping on their beds.

I see Jerusalem as I see my home life: a place that keeps something hidden, that suppresses my desire for openness. There is sometimes sadness, an inexplicable heaviness that permeates my home and spreads in the city. On Geulah Street I see shop owners whose faces express distress mingled with obliviousness, whose plight seems tied with the city's alleys and dusty dead ends.

My father says, Don't tell anybody that I own a building on Amos Street. I don't know why this is a secret and I don't ask. The prohibition fills me with fear: What if someone finds out? My father's tenants come to our door and complain about a water leak or a broken window, and my father tries to accommodate them, worrying that his partner, Goldstein, will object to the expenses involved.

Some of the Bible stories we study in school are cloaked with a secrecy meant to protect the students from knowing a hard truth: that our biblical sages and heroes committed sins and errors, and in spite of their greatness, were life-sized. The sin of King David, sending Uriah the Hittite to die in the front lines of the war in order to take his wife for himself, is explained away. And the sin of King Solomon, marrying a thousand foreign women, is ignored. Rahab, who is clearly described as a whore, and who hid the Israelites on their way to spy on Canaan, is described as a woman who distributes food. (In Hebrew, the root words for whore and food bear a resemblance.)

The mystery of what is not revealed holds a fascination for me. I am curious about the Kabbalah but frightened by the mere mention of the word. We are forbidden to read or even want to read the Kabbalah. It would be like entering the Holy of Holies, seeing God's face. On the Sabbath when the *Kohanim* in the synagogue bless the congregation, I look the other way. No one must see them separating their middle and ring fingers. But someone once showed me that gesture and I secretly practice it.

There are other secrets too. In first grade I attend a Hebrew-speaking school for a year before attending an English girls' school. One day I skip class to register in the new school. This is considered by many as a betrayal of my old school and of the Hebrew language. The next day, when the teacher asks the reason for my absence, I say, following my mothers' instructions, that I had a stomachache. From the corner of the room, another girl who registered in that school says, That's not true, I saw her registering at the English school. I feel the blood rushing to my face. The teacher, with zeal and determination, has the class write a composition about the importance of speaking the Hebrew language. In fact, there is nationwide campaign to this effect, with public signs posted around the city saying: "Speak Hebrew."

In addition to secrets in synagogue and at school, there are secrets about some of the city's buildings. Someone told me that the thin two-story house with small windows near my father's store is a whorehouse. The whores, with red lipstick and low-cut dresses, stand by the windows waving to the British, their smiles and cheerful looks contrasting with the ordinary street. In Givat Shaul, the building that houses the "crazy" feels ominous. The shouting I hear when passing by frightens me, and makes me wonder what the people do in there. I imagine them pacing back and forth in narrow corridors.

Whenever I walk in the neighborhood where the house for the lepers is, I imagine it being part of the biblical story that describes the discrimination against the lepers. I think of the leper in the Bible who had to wear his clothing torn and keep his hair in disarray crying, unclean, unclean. I don't know the exact location of the lepers' house, and I avoid getting close to where I think it is, for fear of catching the disease. I am glad the lepers live apart, although when I read about Miriam, who was struck by leprosy and was confined, I am heartbroken.

There are other buildings that are not fully knowable and that fill me with wonder. In the center of town there is the huge Generali Building. It stands at the intersection of two main streets, Jaffa and Princess Mary. Because of its great height and massive stone structure it overpowers every other building in the area. On its street level there are shops. On its top a lion made of stone spreads its wings. I don't know why he is there and what he represents, but what would Jerusalem be without this lion?

Bezalel Museum, which my parents and I go to on the Sabbath, also captivates me. It is a small museum, the only one in the city. In the garden there is a copy of Michelangelo's *David* in white marble. It has a gentle, permanent presence, always welcoming. Inside, the walls are heavy, and the stone floor is cold and weighty. I am bored looking at the paintings. Still, there is a mystery to the place. An inexplicable wonderfulness.

The YMCA, which houses Christians, looks strangely out of place. It is tall as well as sprawling, and towers above every building in Jerusalem. The lounge is impervious to daylight, with dimly lit chandeliers that hang from its vaulted ceiling. Rumor has it that ham sandwiches are sold there. As I enter, I think it is a forbidden building. I should not walk the halls of taboo food. I have a similar feeling when I go by the Christian bookstore, two streets away. Jolted by the sight of crosses on the covers of the books, I quickly avert my eyes.

Jerusalem is a chastising city. On the Sabbath and Jewish holidays, stores and entertainment houses are closed. Public buses do not run. In ultra-orthodox neighborhoods, modest dress is required at all times. One belongs to a community, and is expected to follow its rules and customs. But in personal matters the city tolerates all kinds of iniquities. It is whispered that a certain teenager has sex with his dog on the roof of his house. And then there are the thieves. Once my father came upon two young men who were trying to rob his store. He recognized them as sons of a neighbor. Their father begged my father not to notify the police, and my father acquiesced.

The city also tolerates uncommon behaviors. The man who has a shoe store in our neighborhood is rumored to be homosexual. Most people including myself like him, and like to buy their shoes from him. The man is patient and courteous. When people mention his homosexuality, they say, It's just one of those things. It is also rumored there are Jewish women who date and even marry British officers. We consider it an anomaly. My parents know a woman whose sister married a British officer and who eventually left for England. I think of her parents and wonder how they reacted to the marriage. And then there is the Nazirite (ascetic) who lives in our midst and who doesn't cut his hair or drink wine. Though we tolerate his asceticism, whenever the subject comes up, we talk in soft voices to conceal our incomprehension and embarrassment.

Our neighborhood, and some of the neighborhoods in the north of Jerusalem around where we live, have unnoteworthy, flat-sounding names. I am embarrassed by the sentimental name of our neighborhood: Yegia Kapaim (Toil of Hands). And the names of other neighborhoods close to ours share a similar sentimental tenor: one to the east is called Achva (Brotherhood), the main street is called Geulah (Redemption), and to the west is a neighborhood called Makor Baruch (The Fountain of Blessing). I admire the names of the streets farther north named after biblical prophets: Amos and Micha reverberate with strength and the beauty of their poetic prophecy, and so do Yonah and Malachi. These streets are also cleaner than ours, and the homes there are more spacious.

When people don't recognize the name of my neighborhood I tell them I live near Schneller, the British army base. Everyone knows Schneller. It is part of our landscape, part of our daily life. Trucks with soldiers entering and leaving the base are a common sight. We say that someone lives "before Schneller," or "after Schneller," or that the bus stop is "in front of Schneller." From our window, we see the clock on top of Schneller's tower, and rely on it for the time. The clock is reassuring. Like a companion who leads you by the hand through difficult hours of the day, the clock never fails; it never fails to show the time.

After World War II, Britain transferred some of its Italian war prisoners to British Mandate Palestine and imprisoned them in Schneller. My girlfriends and I go there to look at the prisoners, who take walks in a big courtyard behind a chain-link fence. The prisoners are cheerful. They smile and we exchange a few words in English. We get to know a few of them, especially Federico. He has black curly hair and an alluring smile. One day my girlfriends and I go to the movies and see him there with a group of other prisoners. We wave to each other and I say, Hi, Federico.

Next to Schneller is a string of shops on Geulah Street, also on the side streets and on Straus Street. Most are specialty stores: the dairy store for eggs and milk, the meat store, the tailor, the dry cleaner, a laundry that washes and irons your linens, the tinsmith, the shoemaker, the pharmacy, the stationery store, the hat store, the clothing store, the fish store, and the shoe store. There is the Mikvah, where we dipped our silverware in water to kosher it before Passover, and the slaughterhouse, where you have your chickens slaughtered after you've proclaimed them the bearers of your sins before Yom Kippur.

There is also the store that sells fabrics. Whenever there is a special occasion like a wedding, you buy fabric for a dress and you hire a dressmaker. The choices are many. As a teenager I enjoy going through the colorful fabrics. If you have a sewing machine, the dressmaker comes to your house and it is a "dressmaker's day" dedicated to sewing and trying on. We don't have a sewing machine, so I must go to the dressmaker's house to try on a dress she is making. After three or four fittings it is ready.

In our neighborhood, as in some others in Jerusalem, there are Ashkenazi, Sephardic, and Yemenite Jews, living side by side on our street. The Ashkenazi Jews say that the Sephardim are lenient regarding their religious observance—they turn on the lights and listen to the radio on the Sabbath. They also say that Sephardic Jews eat rice and beans on Passover, but that it is not a leniency; it is a custom they bring from their home countries. I can't imagine eating rice or beans on Passover, but I am tickled by living next to people who do.

The Sephardic Jews use natural remedies. Sometimes my mother resorts to these remedies. Once, when I have a persistent cough, our Sephardic neighbor Rivka comes to help. Rivka is a large woman with large breasts and large hands. She is very intelligent but illiterate. She has me stretch out on my stomach, and she places cupping glasses on the bare skin of my back. This makes me very uncomfortable, but I remain quiet because Rivka is assured and inspires me with confidence. Another time she places urine-soaked compresses on my leg where I have a rash.

Once, at the age of five, I am sick with a high fever. As my mother is telling me a story, her words die out or become too loud. Her lips are pursed, her skin furrowed. Innocent characters in the story, so familiar to me, change into monsters jumping and bumping into each other. The room spins. I scream. I ask to see Rivka. Her authoritative voice is reassuring. My mother, on the other hand, is small and vulnerable. I want Rivka to sit next to me. I feel her presence would shield me. My mother rushes to get her. I ask Rivka to stay, and she does.

I have a romance with Rivka's family, a brood of eight children—so large compared to my own. Only a low stone fence stands between our terraces and I can hear them conversing in loud voices and shouting at each other. Rivka's five daughters relish taking turns cleaning and scrubbing their house, their terrace, and the stairs that lead up to their apartment. My only household job, which I do reluctantly, is to dust the furniture on Friday morning before the Sabbath. Rivka's children often sit on their terrace and eat salted chickpeas. I love sharing their sweets, their bread dipped in olive oil and sprinkled with *za'atar* (oregano), and their *tremus*, a Mediterranean bean, sprinkled with salt. There is laughter and levity; I admire their vivacity. My family eats its meals in a solemn mood.

Rivka's son Eli is tall and handsome. He is five years older than me, and I have a crush on him. Whenever he sees me going to my piano lesson he asks if he can take me there on his bike. I sit on the crossbar. Sometimes he surprises me and picks me up on my way back. Going down one of the steepest hills in the city is a thrill, especially with his arms closing in on mine. On a few occasions he tries to teach me Ladino. I learn a few words such as *gato* (cat), and phrases such as *keres ir a pasear* (do you want to take a walk). I like to recite them. Eli once tries to show me how he masturbates by manipulating his hand and one finger. He eagerly tries to demonstrate this motion, but I am not interested. It is a boring puzzle. I like to be with him as we stand on each side of the fence that separates our terraces, and simply chat. Every day I look to see if his bike is downstairs by the stairs. It is comforting to see the bike, to know he is home, next to where I stand on the terrace. He has a girlfriend who I think is beautiful. I see them as they come up the stairs to his house. I am jealous. They look grown up and romantic; they know things that I do not.

We have other Sephardic neighbors, too. In the morning the women stand on their terraces and talk to each other in loud voices in Ladino. I don't understand what they are saying, but judging by their animated voices, they must be telling each other very exciting things.

One of our next-door neighbors is a Sephardic couple from Argentina, a rabbi and his wife. We call the wife Rabissa. She sits on her terrace and watches people come and go. She snitches on me to my mother if she doesn't like my "Hello." On most days she waits for mail from her children in Buenos Aires. Every day she talks to her Sephardic neighbors in Ladino about her anticipation, and the neighbors then relate this to my mother in Hebrew. One day her grandson, tall and athletic looking, comes from Buenos Aires for a visit. He lightens Rabissa's heart.

Rabissa and her husband share their apartment with a young Sephardic couple and their two children. The couple eloped when they were seventeen years old, a bone of contention between the young woman and her mother, who lives on the other side of us. The marriage does not work out well. The Ashkenazi neighbors say about the husband, He is very solicitous with his friends and hosts them lavishly, but is not generous with his wife. It is a Sephardic trait.

On the ground floor of our house lives our landlord and his family. He and his wife are from Yemen, and speak to each other in Arabic. The woman makes dishes called *kubeh* and *malawach*. Sometimes the smell from their kitchen is very strong. The Sephardic neighbors say, She burnt her food again; after all, she doesn't have a sense of smell.

Sitting alone at the end of Geulah Street is a large yeshiva with grim, dusty windows. Sometimes when I go by, the genial sun has warmed the cold stone. Sounds of young men learning stream through the windows. When they walk outside with their black coats I think they are still in their own alien world. My father, who supported his family from the age of twelve, says, These people should make a living, and they don't.

The great majority of Ultra-Orthodox Jews, the Haredim, live a few streets away in their own neighborhood, Meah Shearim. When a visitor comes from another town, local people point in that direction and say, This is where the Haredim live. Secular as well as moderately religious people say that the Haredim are radical people with radical ideas about having an independent country, but no one seems to mind them or to take them seriously. I like to go to their neighborhood with my mother to shop in their market. It is a weary, old section where streets are broken, the air is dark, and everyone is poor. The houses and shops are small, and the produce is scarce. There is time to linger and to watch as my mother bargains. She is very comfortable there.

A group that calls itself Neturei Karta (Guardians of the City) lives in Meah Shearim. Their youths throw stones at passing cars that come through their neighborhood on the Sabbath. Most secular people regard these incidents with a shrug. The group is vehemently against the establishment of the State of Israel, believing that the founding of a Jewish state should only happen with the coming of the Messiah. They are on friendly terms with the Arabs, and speak on behalf of their cause.

The long and narrow street that runs through the neighborhood, which is also called Meah Shearim, takes me to my grade school. Among dark-looking stores that sell buttons, fabrics, holy objects, and holy books, there is a pharmacy. Like most pharmacies it has a spacious, well-lit room, clearly labeled bottles organized on shelves, and a pharmacist in a white coat. It amazes me that in the midst of a backward neighborhood of small, cramped houses, with people who are radically religious, there exists a pharmacy.

The city absorbs this tinge of modernism in the midst of extremely traditional practice. It absorbs various ethnic groups with petty resentments towards each other, and it absorbs different centuries-old religions, which, at their highest, are similar in their quest for spirituality. Though burdened by discomfort and restrictions, the city never collapses, not for a moment. Each night it reaches out to its mountainous breezes, takes in fresh, cool air, and is ready to face the next day.

6

A COURTYARD LITTERED WITH ROCKS

In one day a cherished part of my life has vanished. In one day the rich flower garden tended daily by a gardener—a hearty welcome as I walk to my school building, located in Mussrarah, an Arab neighborhood— and the wooden door to the headmistress's office, which we rarely enter, and which is full of mystery, has become only a memory. In one day the clean and orderly and safe courtyard where the students play during recess has become a signal of what's to come, as Arab kids have littered it with rocks thrown over the high, green gate.

I like my school. In gym we dance in pairs to "Where Are You Going My Pretty Maid?" We curtsy, we bow, and we twirl. I like the order in the school, the attention to regularity. Before the first class we march to the music of John Philip Sousa in a big entrance hall. Pictures of King George the VI and his wife, Elizabeth, grace the walls; the headmistress, Miss Landau, a Jewish Orthodox British woman, waves her hand up and down to the rhythm. At the end of recess we line up in the courtyard according to height.

In the geography class the teacher brings us colorful pieces of wool manufactured in Manchester or Birmingham. I imagine these cities to be busy and lively, unlike my city, which repeats its life, always in the grip of solemnity. I have friends in class, but I am still surprised when in third grade the class elects me to be the head girl. For a couple of years I am also chosen by the teachers to be the prefect, overseeing that the students follow the rules. I am not sure how to go about it, but I wear two buttons on my uniform—a blue jumper with a white shirt—that indicate I am in charge.

The classes in English literature and Hebrew literature are taught by the same teacher, who reads "The Highwayman" to us in English, and poems in Hebrew such as Tchernichovsky's poem about King Saul's visit to the witch of Ein-Dor. When she reads "The Highwayman" her voice intermittently rises and falls. In a consistent, dramatic voice she reads the poem describing King Saul's anguish as he knocks on the witch's door furtively in the dark of night. She usually sits on a table in front of the class with her legs apart. The sight of her thighs and slip distracts us, but soon we are carried away by her reading—I can see a silhouette of the Highwayman riding at night, a broad-shouldered, potent man, cloak waving in the wind. And I can see Saul, stooped, un-kingly, anxious to know his predicament.

My mother is pleased I attend this "English" girl's school, named after Evelina de Rothschild, the daughter of a British baron who died in her youth, saying, It is important to learn a foreign language in addition to your native tongue. Every morning we sing the British anthem, and then the Jewish one. As I sing the British anthem, I wonder why we ask God to save the British king. Singing the Jewish anthem evokes a different feeling; the tune and words are melancholic as well as hopeful, which feels like home.

I walk to school, unaccompanied. On my way I see shops open, and people buying bread and milk. I see children hurrying to school, some with uniforms, like myself, others without. I think of the rumor that some Jewish terrorists hide in our neighborhood. I imagine the house they are in, an apartment on a second floor of a street close by. Like most apartments in our neighborhood, it has an external staircase; it also has two doors painted beige. One, I presume, leads to the bathroom or to the kitchen. I imagine the terrorists hiding behind that door, sneaking out in the small hours of the night to sabotage the British.

The "terrorists," as we refer to them, sometimes kill the British, and the British sometimes capture terrorists and hang them. The terrorists' goal is to evict the British who rule the country, so that the Jews can gain independence. At school or with my friends we never talk about the terrorists. At home my father talks about them with trepidation. I often see pictures of the captured terrorists on the front page of the newspaper. I also keep hearing the voice of Geulah Cohen, the illegal Lehi station announcer, and I imagine an isolated woman raging against the British, hidden in a cubicle. She inspires fear in me. What is it like to be wanted and in hiding? How does she manage food and sleep without ever venturing out, I wonder.

The terrorists belong to two groups: Etzel (National Military Organization in the Land of Israel), and Lehi (Fighters for the Freedom of Israel), a radical underground group that splintered off from Etzel. Etzel aims to settle the entire land of Palestine, including Jordan, with Jews. I think it is an infantile and grandiose dream. What are they going to do with the Arabs? Their logo is scary: the words Rak Kach (Only Thus) alongside a hand holding a rifle, superimposed on a map of two banks of the Jordan River. Their secret identity is well guarded. I am at once intrigued by them and disparaging of their brazen, violent acts.

Decisions about the fate of the terrorists who are captured take place on the outskirts of the city, at the British High Commissioner's house that stands on a hill. From afar it looks like a sharp-angled house without ornament. But I am told that it has domed roofs and a formal garden. When an order comes out from this house, there is nothing in the world that will change it. Sometimes there is talk about the High Commissioner pardoning a terrorist who kills or plans to kill British soldiers, but I don't believe this has ever happened.

One of the terrorists was captured in Makor Baruch, a neighborhood I walk by on the way to my recorder lessons. The proximity of the house he was captured in excites me. How and where exactly was he captured? I keep imagining the street, the house, soldiers surrounding the house, and a brave young man desperately attempting to escape.

I like carrying my recorder, and I like playing it, especially familiar tunes. The sound of my recorder is unassuming. I play a song about Alissa and her goat and have visions of a meadow, grass. The lessons are intimate. Quiet. I play for my teacher, and she plays for me. I enjoy the attention given by her, not to my health or my looks, which my mother lavishes on me, but to my playing.

Playing the recorder whets my appetite. Now I want to play the piano. I persist in asking my mother for piano lessons. My uncle in New York sends me a piano, and when my piano arrives the neighbors look on from their terraces as the carriers haul it up the stairs. We place the piano in the living room. The room loses its simplicity. It is more than itself. My piano teacher, Mrs. Kurkidi, a big woman with large hands, is loud and gregarious. Her fingernails are long, painted red, and when she plays she seems oblivious to the clicking sound her nails make on the keys. I practice the piano every day. On one occasion my teacher pairs me up with a boy two years older than me to play four hands. The boy is blond, with freckles on his face. I like him. But he is indifferent towards me, doesn't even speak to or look at me. Once, we play in a small concert hall in Rehavia, an elegant neighborhood, for an audience of family and friends. My nose drips and I am very uncomfortable. The audience applauds, we bow, and I see my mother in one of the front rows, smiling.

But generally my mother is not interested in my playing, nor is she interested in music. But she likes to sing when she works in the kitchen. When my school friends visit me, and my mother's voice rings in the house with "Daisy, Daisy" and "You Are My Sunshine," I am embarrassed, and wish my mother didn't sing in English. I also wish she spoke Hebrew without mistakes. For many years my mother did not read Hebrew newspapers. From the time she arrived in Israel, she would read *Reader's Digest* and *Life*, which her family, with whom she is always corresponding, sends her.

My mother's first languages are Yiddish, Polish, and then English. She speaks Yiddish with my father, but to me she speaks in Hebrew. Hebrew is my language, the desirable language in this country. I idealize it. Even idolize it. We, the young generation, all do. My mother's spelling mistakes in Hebrew are of help to my father. Whenever his customers, some of whom are immigrants from Europe, fill out orders, my mother is able to decipher their Hebrew, mistakes and all.

My mother is also able to speak to British officers who routinely search business places for hidden and undeclared merchandise. The British Mandate that rules the city preserves law and order and prevents crime, and they come to my father's store without warning. My mother, who enjoys chatting with people, captures their attention—they seem eager to have a conversation with someone who speaks English.

Once, after a search, a British officer—thin, tall, and red-faced—asks my mother out for tea. My father motions to my mother that it's okay, and my mother tells me to come along. We go to Café Vienna, two blocks away. The café is a big, half-circled room. Floor tiles are black and white, and the tables are small and round. As we enter I am embarrassed, and wonder if people are looking at us. The British officer is very polite and pulls out a chair out for my mother to sit on. We have tea in shiny cups and saucers, as my mother and the officer chat. It dawns on me that I am my mother's chaperone.

Another time, two English officers come to search our apartment. After they complete the search they point to a door high on a wall and want to know where it leads. It's the door to our attic. My mother brings a ladder and encourages them to climb up. One officer, attempting to enter the attic, hits his head on the low ceiling and soon climbs down. Whenever my mother tells this story she laughs with glee.

As part of preserving order, the British impose curfews to prevent violence after the hanging of a Jewish terrorist. We've had many curfews. When they are announced, British troops patrol the city and roll out barbed-wire barricades. We call the soldiers *Kalaniot* (anemones) because of their red berets and what we believe to be their black hearts. During a curfew the city is eerily silent; it accepts the decree, and waits anxiously for news. One day, it is rumored that a member of Etzel, captured after an explosion at the city's rail station, will be hanged. The execution of a member of Lehi, caught with a hand grenade a few blocks away from our house, will take place at the same time.

Later, the city shudders with yet another daring act of these two prisoners. Hand grenades, placed in hollowed-out oranges, are smuggled to them before they are to be executed. The two commit suicide in their jail cell by placing the grenades between their bodies and igniting them with a cigarette. (Their original plan was to hurl the grenades at the hangman, but when they learned there would be a rabbi attending the execution, they changed their plan.) The city is grayer than usual. The air is filled with unanswered questions. There is shock, and deep grief. The pictures of the two are in the paper. I am drawn to the photos, thinking of the bold and mysterious act of these two men. Then I recoil. I look again. The dark eyes of the Lehi guy look straight at me. A shiver goes through my body.

In retaliation for the execution of three Jewish terrorists, Etzel members kill two British soldiers and then hang them. I imagine the soldiers hanging from eucalyptus trees in an orchard near Netanya, their heads limp, their bodies lifeless. The hanging of Jews, although it horrifies us and leaves us shocked, has become part of our lives. But the hanging of British soldiers is so unexpected it leaves us dumbfounded.

Most people say the terrorists are reckless and their actions are appalling. Others admire them for their fearlessness and refer to them as freedom fighters. Still others retort that they only make trouble, and if it weren't for their actions the city would be peaceful. As it is, the city cannot do anything to stop the terrorism or the hangings. But it takes comfort in knowing that Rabbi Aryeh Levin visits the terrorists when they are jailed. Levin is known for visiting the sick and sitting by their beds for hours, among them lepers in Bethlehem who are mostly Arabs. The prisoners are grateful for his presence and the respect he shows them. Everyone admires his loving-kindness and courage and thinks he is a *tzaddik* (a righteous man). I once saw his picture in the newspaper and was surprised he looked like an ordinary man. People say that he talks to the terrorists before they are hanged. I wonder what he says to them.

As I play on the terrace with my neighbor one day, Etzel bombs the King David Hotel. Suddenly the floor underneath us shakes. I thrill to hear the story of how the Etzel members entered the hotel disguising themselves as Arab milkmen, hiding the bombs in large milk containers. But the thrill is mingled with fear that the disguise might have been discovered. People are very upset because they say many innocent people were killed. I don't understand why these people are innocent and the British soldiers are not. I also don't understand why the British are prepared to die in order to rule this country.

Finally, the British have had enough. They declare that their mandate over Palestine will end. The United Nations votes for the Partition of Palestine, a plan that divides the land between the Jews and the Arabs. The Arabs reject the U.N. plan. Riots erupt. People say Arabs are rioting on Princess Mary Street with the aim of killing Jews. I imagine throngs of enraged Arabs with heavy sticks leaving the Old City and climbing the hilly street, shouting. The idea of a face-to-face confrontation with them scares me. Etzel plants a bomb at Damascus Gate in the Old City, killing many people.

My school closes immediately after the Arab kids throw rocks over the high, green gate into the courtyard. Arabs are engaged in acts of violence across the country. They have objected to the Zionists building a home-land for the Jews, even though Jews have been immigrating to Palestine for decades. They have resented them for violating their rights to the land they have lived on for centuries. As early as 1929 the Arabs have occasionally attacked Jews. When my father talks about the massacre of Jews that year in Hebron, he is dismayed and incredulous: How could Arabs, who have been the neighbors of Jews for decades, one day turn on them and murder them? My father chats with his Arab customers in Arabic. They are friendly and pleasant. I especially like the hospitality of one Arab customer when we visited his home. They also have a reputa-tion for putting a knife in your back, as they did in the Hebron massacre. My father thinks they are honest businessmen, but he, too, believes that they might turn on you without warning.

Once, in a taxi with my parents riding from Tel Aviv to Jerusalem, we hear shots. The driver takes a side road. Everyone in the taxi is silent and fearful. I look back and see a man lying face down in a dirt field. There is heat and dust and the man is motionless. My mother turns my head away. I think the man must be dead. Someone in the taxi says he is an Arab.

Two bombings, one after another, shake up Jerusalem. One night, a bomb explodes at the offices of *The Palestine Post,* the Jewish-owned, English language daily newspaper. Many say the British carried it out. Some blame the Arabs. The next day, a truck explodes on Ben Yehuda Street, killing many people and destroying buildings, a collaborative act of the Arabs and the British. Our shock and resentment deepens.

In 1947, the U.N. declares the establishment of the State of Israel for the Jews, next to a Palestinian state for the Arabs. I think the countries that voted for this are very nice. Everyone is happy and goes dancing in the streets. But I am sad about the "green line" that will separate the Arabs and the Jews.

May 14, 1948. The day the British Mandate ends and the Israeli Declaration of Independence is proclaimed, thousands of people pour into the streets and dance. The mood is ebullient. But my father is worried. Growing up under Turkish rule and experiencing their lack of concern about the city and its citizens made him see the British as redeemers. On one hand, he fears that without the law and order they enforce, the country will return to chaos. (Like most people, I am enthused about having an independent country and I am embarrassed by my father's attitude.) On the other, he credits and admires "the untrustworthy and hot-blooded terrorist organizations," as he calls them, for driving out the British. I am left to wonder how a group can be untrustworthy and still affect things positively.

The celebratory mood doesn't last. Israel is attacked by all the surrounding Arab countries. My father is glued to the radio and he tells my mother and I the dreadful news: Syria, Lebanon, and Iraq are attacking Israel in the north. Egypt is attacking in the south. The Arab Legion of Jordan is attacking Jerusalem. I imagine the Arab armies comprised of fearless and gigantic soldiers who are well armed, approaching the north and the south and marching towards Jerusalem. In Latrun, midway between Tel Aviv and Jerusalem, the Jordanians blockade the road to Jerusalem. The city is now surrounded by them and is bombarded with mortar shells.

Upon the first attack we go, to be safe, to the ground floor where our landlady lives. Suddenly the sound of a mortar shell jolts us, and my neighbor, a girl my age, and I, pee on the bed we are sitting on. It is mortifying to have this happen to me and on somebody else's bed. The landlady gives our family an unused room with one window, which we stuff with sandbags. My grandmother and two aunts, who live farther away from the line of attack, are afraid to stay on their own, and move in to live with us. The six of us sleep on mattresses on the floor. I sleep between my aunts and my parents. In the corner of the room is a brown square chair with some dishes and cups on it, and a small shelf with a pack of oatmeal. A kerosene stove to cook on is in the courtyard. We share a toilet in the courtyard with the landlady's family. There is very little talk about the war.

We live in the north of Jerusalem, not very far from where the Arab Legion is attacking. Mortar shells continue to rain on us. I don't think of being injured or killed, or who will win the war. I am just frightened by the sound of artillery. When a mortar shell is fired I hear a muffled, distant sound and then a shrill whistle. I cover my ears so as not to be jolted by the sound of the exploding shell.

Sandbags protect all the windows on our street. But in spite of this, shrapnel penetrates through the window of a house next door and kills a child. People whisper about it in disbelief. In another incident, mortar shells go through the roof of the house on our right and the roof of the house on our left. My family says it is a miracle that a mortar shell didn't hit our roof. It is odd, I think, that what is a tragedy for one is a miracle for another.

We are under siege. The water pipeline has been blown up. People use rationed water from cisterns, and sometimes I see a line by the cistern in our courtyard. No one smiles. No one complains. Everyone is anxious to survive, looking for food and water, and protecting themselves from the shelling.

During the siege I never go out; the city is invisible to me. My mother and our female neighbors collect weeds in the fields. They make different dishes from the weeds—soups, patties, and salads. My mother sometimes goes to buy food in the neighborhood but often comes back empty-handed. She tells us, The streets were empty, mortar shells were falling, but it seems I ran between them.

My father is recruited to serve in Mishmar Ha'am, a civilian defense unit. Every day he leaves to guard a makeshift gate in our neighborhood, making sure that whoever enters or leaves is legitimate. I feel shame that he is not a soldier, fighting, that he wears a civilian uniform, a khaki hat whose brim is floppy, not the tight beret with a military emblem. I think my father is a coward, shirking his duty—a cardinal sin in a land that depends on ideals such as sacrifice and a fighting spirit for its existence. And I hate him for that. (Later when I serve in the army and work on a kibbutz, fellow soldiers treat with contempt anybody who tries to avoid training or work.) I do not know something my father reveals to me years later, inadvertently: that he was blind in one eye and hence was excused from active duty.

All schools in Jerusalem are closed. My girlfriend Ada and I decide to start a school in our landlady's big room for the little children living in our street. We gather a few children and schedule classes in Hebrew, math, and history. We ring a bell at the beginning and at end of classes. After school Ada and I play with dolls. I am glad I have my doll carriage so we can wheel our dolls around.

Young people take part in the war. A seventeen-year-old girl runs through the streets of Jerusalem passing notes to the army stationed in the north and is hit by shrapnel. Doctors amputate her arm. I keep imagining her running without fear or hesitation, and wonder how she gets along without an arm. My neighbor Eli, who used to take me on his bike, is now a sniper stationed in Notre Dame between the Old City and the new, facing the Arab Legion. He comes home only briefly, and greets me, but doesn't have time to talk to me. I imagine him on that high building, concentrating on perfect aim. He will always be my secret love, my secret hero.

Miraculously, a convoy of supplies arrives from Tel Aviv on a newly built road that goes through the far hills called Burma Road. A paratrooper, the son of a distant relative of my father from Tel Aviv, comes to our house and brings eggs and other kinds of food. My parents are delighted and very surprised, and everyone showers him with blessings. I stand in the courtyard and stare at him. He is so brave and handsome with his khaki clothes and red beret. How did he find us? We have never even heard of him. He might as well have descended from the sky.

The siege ends, and the war in other parts of the country ends, too. In our wartime school we have a party for the parents and children. The children stage a play and sing songs, and I am sad about the end of the school.

To recuperate from the war, my father decides to move to a town near Tel Aviv. We stay with friends for a few months. The town, not touched by the war, is in central Israel. People are at ease. The houses built with stucco seem weightless, unlike houses in Jerusalem with their massive stone facades. It is fall and the air is warm. I adapt to my new school, feeling embraced by the teacher and my new friends. Coming from the enduring city of Jerusalem makes me sort of a celebrity. My knowledge of English helps: in an outdoor celebration I am picked to greet the new U.S. ambassador to Israel, who visits our school, with all the students attending. Sabbaths are devoted to the activities of Bnei-Akiva, the religious youth movement I am a member of. We sit in a circle and sing songs about our love for the land. Saturday nights we sometimes dance to tango music coming from a gramophone. I dance with a fifteen-year-old boy, who draws my body close to his chest; I feel a sudden stirring, a melting—all combined. I forget the war.

7

IN THE HIDDENNESS OF SCHNELLER WOODS

Upon our return to Jerusalem my father reopens his store. His old customers return. I feel proud, less for Israel's victory than for the political independence we have achieved. I now discover, to my shock, that our next door neighbor Shalom, was a member of Lehi at age thirteen, mining roads to blow up British military vehicles before the war. The story about the "Davidka," the noisy mobile mortar that led the Arabs to believe we had more artillery than we did, is a favorite of mine. I like to visit the mortar, which was placed as a monument in an intersection of streets not far from my house.

Almost immediately, we have our own army, our own money. We say, This is the only place we will ever live in and love. So much of what was British and Arab is gone: the pictorial stamps of Palestine issued under the British Mandate are replaced with stamps issued by the Israeli government, and some street signs with British names are replaced by signs with names of Jewish heroes and notables. The city is energetic. I often hear construction workers shouting *barud*—the warning call before quarrying stone—the sound of explosion immediately after, and the sound of hammering and chiseling of the stone intended for new buildings.

My parents install a device to heat the water electrically, replacing our old wood burning heater. The policeman in the center of town who directed traffic has been replaced by a traffic light, the only traffic light in the city. Our neighbor Leah has begun working as a stewardess for El Al, our country's new airline. Before flights she stands on her terrace sipping black coffee and smoking a cigarette. She wears her airline uniform; her hair is cropped. Wide-eyed I watch her put her shiny lipstick on. The worldliness of other countries has already touched her, and she carries this to our modest neighborhood.

But underneath the quick recovery attesting to the city's resilience, I sense a penetrating remembrance of having endured a war that threatened to annihilate us, and a deepening feeling of loss. The Old City is lost to the Arabs. There are thousands of fallen soldiers. A family across the street from us lost two young sons. I keep picturing one of them, Avner, blond, with a muscular body and a well-defined face; he made me think of the biblical Avner, a figure I love, who attempted to unite the factions of the two kings, Saul and David, and was slain in the process.

The city begins to expand, but it is also under rules of austerity. Food and even shoes and furniture are rationed. Dov Yosef, the man who runs the austerity plan, is considered a tyrant. His name is on everyone's lips, and I shudder at the mere sound of it. My mother is in search of nutritious food, and being generally blasé about rules, especially when it comes to my health and well-being, she buys black-market eggs and butter. A classmate's mother tells her she never buys food on the black market. My mother says of this woman, Her son became very ill because of malnutrition; I don't understand how a mother can deprive her child of food just because of some rules.

The camp in Schneller is now in the hands of the Israeli army. I see Israeli soldiers, casually hatless, leaving and entering the camp. The tower clock no longer works. The hands look limp and beaten, the color of the tower washed out, like an ancient ruin that once held some importance. It saddens me that the Arab owners of the mansion across the street from Schneller have abandoned their house and left. Before the war, their garden bloomed and the fishpond had water, and on a sunny day the water sparkled and the goldfish darted back and forth. We children would come and look through the bars of their iron fence, marveling at the sight of it all. Now there is no water in the fishpond and the grass and trees are untended.

Walls and barbed-wire fences now separate us from the Arabs. We can no longer mingle with them in the Old City, nor can we mingle with the Armenian monks in their long black robes. Jericho, my beloved town, with her palm trees and her holy spring, is behind lines. The Arabs can no longer come from the Old City of Jerusalem to the new to trade in the market, and we cannot go to their market. The Arab wearing a *keffiyeh* (a traditional headdress worn by Arabs), who, along with his goat, came daily to the field across from our house, no longer comes, and my mother no longer stands in line and waits for him to milk his goat into her small aluminum pot. The exchange between them was businesslike, but it was also close, as if they belonged to one family.

I take piano lessons from Miss Eshet, who recently arrived from Eastern Europe. Miss Eshet is a kindly woman, a divorcee. She lives alone. I am very fond of her, and I think she found a friend in me. We develop an emotional bond. I am enamored of her brilliant piano playing and make sure to listen to whenever she performs on the radio. Her house in Talpiot Haktana, which borders Arab territory, is punctured with bullet holes. After the piano lessons she and I have coffee by the window. I gaze, numbly, at a barbed-wire fence and a stretch of no-man's land over-grown with thorns. Below, in an Arab village, an Arab sits on a flat roof; another rides a donkey on a narrow path. Our lives go on separately.

I often feel tense about the barriers. I think the people who live on the other side of the border behind Mandelbaum Gate are tense about them, too. I never go by Mandelbaum Gate, which is not a gate, but a border crossing between the Jewish and Arab parts of the city manned by the United Nations. There are rules and regulations about travel to the other side, and one needs a permit. The Gate is named after the family who lived in the house next to the Gate before the war. After the war the family, who own a lingerie store in the center of town, moved. Their name has an ominous sound: a reminder of the war, and of the enemy who lives in proximity. But it also has a warm sound, reminiscent of the time before the war, when the family lived peacefully among the Arabs.

I attend a new school, a co-ed modern religious school, Ma'aleh. The boys have to wear yarmulkes and pray every morning. Girls are exempt. The school stresses academic studies. The strong presence of boys and male teachers give the school a masculine and demanding tone. The school is Israeli in character, with an emphasis on Hebrew, so different from my former Jewish-British girls' school, where the official language was English, and where style and play were important ingredients.

The way to my new school, with its winding streets and quaint buildings, is in contrast to the way to my old school was—now in no-man's
land—a long, straight road with the broken sidewalks of an ultra-
religious neighborhood, and then through a street with Arab stores,
colorful carpets hanging on the walls and brass jugs and cups displayed
on brass tables. I enjoy the new way: the smell emitted by a small
bakery, a big and long room with ovens that seem magical, with bakers
immersed in their work; houses, small and unassuming, on one a sign
that says "piano tuner," an Abyssinian church with big gates, the dome
always aglow, and priests strolling in a well-tended garden; the titillating
window of a well-known author of erotic novels, who lives on the corner;
another street, this one in shadows, the buildings with interior staircases,
and people coming and going among the shadows, meditative, deep in
thought, away from my street, which faces a wide glaring sun that drives
any wrongdoing out of hiding.

I enjoy socializing and having girlfriends in school. But I am haughty
towards the boys. I ignore them. Later I would shudder at having felt
distant when I heard, a year after graduation, that Dan, the brilliant,
most gifted boy in our class, was killed in army training. His face was
mischievous and beguiling. I regret not knowing him better.

I also ignore some of the girls. One of them is Carmela, who, it was rumored, committed suicide upon graduating from high school by jumping
from a moving truck. She was a loner. I don't remember her ever talking
with anyone. When I think about it years later I cannot believe that an act
so grave evoked so little thought or feeling on my part. I felt no horror,
not even a morbid curiosity. Hearing about her suicide was stepping into
an uncharted sea, with only an image of her blond hair ruffled by a wind
as she leapt to her death.

My classmates and I recite passages from the Bible by heart. Many of the
biblical heroes are my heroes, army commanders like Joshua, or Ehud,
or Gideon—blessed and triumphant until the end. Ehud, the son of Gera,
who kills Eglon the King of Moab, especially intrigues me. I envision
the upper room of the king covered with red carpets, the king himself

dressed in gold; Ehud as shrewd and quick and fearless, swiftly using his left hand, unexpectedly, to pull his dagger from under his clothes, over his right thigh, to kill the king. When I read about kings and warriors who took risks and also broke Jewish law, a tiny voice I barely hear, maybe just a feeling or a sense deep within me, longs to break out and express something not in conformity with my home or my community.

Biblical heroines incur my envy, especially Deborah, a judge and a warrior. I could see her sitting under Deborah's Palm tree in the highlands of Ephraim, and I cannot imagine any of us girls as tough and as resilient and wise as she. She served as Israel's judge when no man was willing to lead. And she led men to war without hesitation. We recite her bold, unapologetic war song. We also recite King Saul's words before he dies. Poor King Saul, despairing, favored, and destroyed, communing with spirits both sorcerous and divine.

I think of Jacob! I don't question his stealing of Esau's birthright. Jacob is forever lonely, burdened by his legacy, forever struggling with his destiny, his love for Rachel, and battling with the angel, lamenting the loss of Joseph, his favorite son. And I imagine Abraham leaving behind his family and country and wandering. I am touched by his covenant with God—the darkness and the terror he experiences. In comparison, my fears are about such trifles: harsh words, big beetles, cats that jump out of garbage cans at night. I am also struck by Abraham's extent of sympathy: "During the hottest part of the day" he runs to greet the angels who appear to him as regular men, perhaps even heathen; he runs from the entrance of his tent to meet them and bows to the ground; he rushes his wife Sara to make loaves of bread for them, serving them a tender calf his servant has prepared, and cream and milk. Abraham's hospitality, the instant trust he has in his guests, his unreserved, accommodating welcome, evoke in me, each time I read the story, a visceral, eye-opening response.

The stories in the Bible that have to do with sex arouse in me more than a regular curiosity: The story about Amnon, who sexually violates his sister Tamar, and the story about another woman named Tamar, who, without betraying any guilt or shame, disguises herself as a harlot and seduces her father-in-law Judah (after his two sons to whom she was married had died), in order to have his descendant as a child.

Many of my conversations with my girlfriends, Dina and Rina, revolve around sex. We talk about each other's bodies, the size of our breasts and hips, whether we need to wear a bra or not. When my girlfriends and I dance with boys and they put their hands on our backs, we suspect the touch of their hands is meant to detect whether or not we wear a bra. In the hiddenness of Schneller Woods near my house, Dina, Rina, and I excitedly peruse a book that discusses sex. We name the sexual organs with letters from the Greek alphabet: *epsilon* for penis, *lamda* for vagina, and *omega* for breasts. On the way home from school, we stop at a kiosk and take turns asking the owner, with a straight face, if he has epsilon, or lamda, or omega, while the rest of us stand a little farther away and laugh and laugh.

I stealthily read the lewd sections of *The Decameron,* stacked in the corner of the bottom shelf of our bookcase at home. I discover my body, my desire. Friday nights when my parents go to visit their friends, I enjoy the stillness in the house, the dim lights in the rooms, the keen aloneness. In my parents' bedroom, on the inside of their wardrobe door, is a big mirror; I open the door of the wardrobe and undress, and stand naked and look at myself, and kiss the reflected lips in the mirror.

My girlfriends and I are restless. We want adventure. We defy rules. We sneak into theatrical performances, like the one that features Yvonne De Carlo. She sings, holding a microphone, revealing her legs through slits in her dress while walking on the stage. I am astonished that she, a Hollywood star, came all the way to the Edison Theater to sing for us. Once, we climb a fence and steal flowers from the rose garden of the Belgian consulate, which had opened in the south of the city. When we go by that building, we point and say, This is where the consulate is. Having a consulate in our midst feels like an infringement.

We take to calling out our desires on the streets of Jerusalem. Rina is in love with our English teacher. She also has a crush on a man whom we frequently see on a terrace on our way home from the youth movement.

At night we stand by the teacher's house, yelling repeatedly, Mr. Chain! Rina is in love with you. No one responds. The night, the shadows, the garden fence behind which we hide, nothing stirs. Hiding behind a wall of a building, we also shout at the man who putters on his terrace in his sleeveless undershirt, You, the guy with the blue eyes, the girl with the red collar is in love with you. Our voices ring out in the clear evening air of Jerusalem. It doesn't matter that there is no response. We know "blue-eyes" is unattainable.

So much of what happens is a subject for fun. We giggle a great deal. We whisper about our math teacher, who has a reputation for touching the girls in school, and who once had me stand against the wall, his arms pressed to the wall on both sides telling me I was intelligent and asking me why I was not doing better in math. I kept thinking I wanted to wrest myself out of his trap, though there was something flattering about his perverse attention.

Dina, Rina, and I meet Jacques after seeing him in a show by the musical troop "Lee Lah Loh," in which he is the accordion player. We pass him a note that says we would like to meet him after the show. It is miraculous that he agrees. He walks with us with the confidence of one who is used to being picked up by girls. He wears a long navy coat with the collar turned up. We hang on every word he says, we admire his every feature, the tiny lines around the mouth when he smiles, revealing he has had many experiences with girls, the mischievous spark in his eyes, a bit of a swagger in his walk, his black, curly hair that shines in the dark night. For months afterward we are lovesick. We compose a song about how dear he is to us, almost as dear as Clark Gable in *Gone with the Wind*. Perhaps even dearer.

Once a week Tzvi and I go to the movies. He picks me up in early evening, and after the movie he walks me home. I met Tzvi at a Purim party after school, when he, handsome and popular among the girls, invites me to dance with him. I think I stand out because of the costume I wear of an Arab woman, an embroidered dress and a beaded necklace on my forehead. As he stands by the piano, Tzvi sings about longing for a woman. He looks at me. Later, as we walk in the school courtyard, Tzvi asks me to be his girlfriend. Of all the girls, he asks me. I fidget with the small comb in the pocket of my dress, breaking one tooth after another. The next day while doing my homework I feel light-headed, my mind wanders, the notebook lies open on my desk, and I cannot study. My body does not feel like my body, which is usually quiet; my body wants to be elsewhere, it is drawn out of itself and wants to be elsewhere.

A whirlwind. I am swept up in a vortex of boys. I have a crush on a boy, and soon after on another. Danny is tall and blond, and I watch him play basketball at the YMCA, watch every move of his, wait for a glance, wait for a sign, though I know he doesn't know I exist. I stare at boys and they stare at me. It is flattering to be looked at. The men from the tax building across from our school look from their windows at the girls' gym classes that take place in the courtyard. One young man, I am told, is looking at me. Why is he looking at me?

Once a year in summer, we go on strenuous hikes dressed in khaki, walking boots, and puttees wound around our ankles, as part of the pre-army training group called Gadna. It is forbidden to drink water while hiking, but we don't complain. We are eager to prove our strength. We are eager to traverse the land, claiming it as our own. Once, along the way to the hiking route in the north of the country, we pass Ra'anana and Kefar Saba, Jewish settlements with orchards and small houses surrounded by trees and plants. We also pass Arab villages, houses with flat roofs scattered along narrow paths, with only a few trees. Many of these villages are built on hills or on mountains. They seem wanting, lacking in energy, their minarets like fading memories. I relate to these villages the way I relate to Bedouin camps in the Negev—turning away from what seems to be extreme neglect. But sometimes a certain village lures me. Though the houses are built in a disorderly fashion, they seem anchored, exuding a warm spirit. It is summer and the air is damp and relaxed. The hike is demanding. We walk under a blasting sun through valleys and we climb high mountains, often for many hours a day. In spite of continuous fatigue our spirits are high. We train to endure, and we do.

Also in summer I work on a religious kibbutz as part of a program devised by our youth movement, Tzofim Datiyim (Religious Scouts), and as scouts, we have no political affiliation. Other youth movements in Jerusalem range politically from the left to the right. The members of those on the extreme left wear blue shirts. Those on the extreme right wear brown shirts and their faces are grim, sometimes they look angry. During summer camp we work in the orchard, picking grapes. Once, in the evening, as we dance the hora, I stare at Shaul, a counselor, and I think he stares at me. The next day I search for him among the faces of everyone. (The feeling of unrequited longing has become familiar, but no less aching.) I look for him across the orchard where I pick grapes. The sun blazes, grapes glisten. Sweat from my forehead falls to the ground. Will he be approaching from the path? Our group stages a play, a bit of a love story. During rehearsals there is a question of whether to allow the main characters, a boy and a girl, to kiss, and it is finally decided that they will stand behind a cloth screen, and as they come closer to each other their shadows will touch as if they were kissing.

As part of a drive to develop a dialogue between teenage members of religious youth movements and non-religious ones, I correspond with Ruth, a member of a secular, left-wing youth movement. In one of my letters I write adamantly about the importance of keeping the command-ment not to eat pork. Jews were martyred for this reason, I add, Hannah and her seven sons were murdered by the Romans for their refusal to eat pork. One Sabbath I visit Ruth in Tel Aviv. I feel nervous when her father, Avraham Shlonski, a major poet, answers my knock and opens the door. He is thin, wearing plain clothes. Why didn't you ring the bell? Because it is the Sabbath, I reply. He doesn't respond; his eyes behind glasses are distracted. Ruth and I visit the gathering place of her movement, the "nest," as they call it. I imagine that the blue color of their uniform stands for their socialist beliefs. That's true idealism, I think. It sends a message of strength and of justice, and even of valor. The message of our youth movement feels meek by contrast. It invites images of learning, and of scripture, and of dull rooms with old-fashioned desks and chairs.

I don't know whether my desire for privacy comes from living in a tight community or from sharing narrow quarters with my parents. I long for my own room and my own desk, a place that would afford me immer-sion in writing a journal. I imagine that one day, when I am married, I will have a room of my own, a writing desk with drawers filled with my private possessions. I'll write about things that are hushed deep inside me. None of my close girlfriends have their own room. One classmate of mine is an exception. Her mother is from New York; her parents are said to be wealthy. I am enamored of her room with its light blue chiffon curtains and a bedspread to match.

I long for anything original, individual, that has an opinion that dissents from what I feel is inert thinking. I am glad to learn that Ahad-Ha'am, the Jewish writer and philosopher, had the courage to be critical of the Jewish settlements of the first Zionists, believing that the Arabs will eventually resist them. I listen with curiosity to Gilbert and Sullivan records, the songs from *The Mikado* played for us by our English teacher from Britain, who looks pathetically lonely in his mad enthusiasm for this music, which is so different from the patriotic or romantic songs we are accustomed to. Yeshayahu Leibowitz, my chemistry teacher, is a renowned scientist and philosopher. As an Orthodox Jew and a writer on religious thought he intrigues me, because he boldly declares his dissension from several common religious thoughts such as his belief in the separation of state and religion. And though Aldous Huxley's essays have a chill to them, and Jane Austen's world is too fastidious and exclusive to afford a feeling of intimacy, I enjoy that difference, that very difference.

I feel privileged to study Talmud, thrilled I am good at a subject traditionally reserved for boys. I like studying the Mishna, a book full of quasi-poetic religious details: where to build the Sukkah, or where to look or not look for *hametz* (leavened bread, or anything made of leavened dough, prohibited to eat or possess on Passover), and what a congregation does if the first winter month has come and no rain had fallen. My studies are slightly interrupted when I once refuse to see my Mishna teacher, who is married, outside the school hours.

The longing for "something else" persists, for something less monotonous and less conforming than my city, something that will lift me above my weary street. Something that will invigorate my life, mark me as someone different. One afternoon I open a door to a classroom of my high school (used by a music school in the afternoon), and I see a man playing the piano and a woman leaning over it. The man has thoughtful eyes. He is immersed in the music and intermittently looks longingly at the woman, and she at him. I think, This is what I want to do, music.

8

IN UNIFORM, IN LOVE

The room I am in is dull and impersonal. The testers wear army uniforms. I have enlisted in the Nachal Brigade—fighting pioneer youth—a unit in the army formed by various youth movements that trains and also works on a kibbutz. My group, which consists of fifty men and women from the "movement," is required to take a multiple-choice aptitude test, the kind of which that is unknown to me. The pressure to choose the correct answer among several possible answers blocks my mind. I am overwhelmed, helpless. I numbly check circles here and there. I don't really know what I am doing. Everyone else seems to know what to do. I see some people walking out of the room confidently. I am still bent over my test, feeling anxious, until the time is up. When I get on the bus to leave for the base, the helplessness lifts. I look forward to be on my own, away from home. I see my mother waving to me. She did not object to my going to the army, although I qualify for an exemption as a woman who practices Orthodox Judaism (a few of my girlfriends stayed out of the army for this reason). But her smile is ambivalent, and her eyes reveal a tender longing.

Our training base is near Tel Aviv; it used to house the British. The girls in my group live in old cement barracks. Our room is very long, with many beds on each side. The platoon sergeant teaches us to make our beds in proper military fashion, with sheets and blankets tucked neatly and firmly under the mattress. We are ordered to keep the room dust-free. Each day the officer in charge makes her morning rounds. We stand at attention while she checks to see whether our beds are properly made and runs her finger across the windowsills to see if there is any dust. Her grave look is out of proportion to her task, and on one occasion my girlfriend Ruth and I burst into a nonstop giggle. As a result, we are ordered to water the trees on the base. That night, in a frivolous mood, we fill pails with water, lug them through the barracks and water every tree in sight.

Mornings, we stand in formation and train. We also train in the afternoon. Blankness permeates the barracks, the trees, and the sky. We are constantly told what to do, do this and that, but the orders do not weigh on me. There is nothing emotional or mean about them, they are plainly spoken and clear. Sometimes I think the orders are comical—it is funny to be ordered to dust windowsills or to stand at attention while our sergeant walks amongst us, inspecting our uniforms. We are taught to care for our rifles—take them apart, clean, and reassemble them. We sit under a tree, my girlfriends and I, and I follow the instructor's words. I merely do what she says to do with this rifle that has no meaning to me. And yet sitting under a tree with my friends, and with the instructor whose voice is calm under a cloudless October sky, the ground mostly bare and flat, I have a sense of pride, a modest pride, about this new autonomy that belongs to being here, away from the constraints of my home in Jerusalem. Although the days are filled with orders that I follow, I have a sense of freedom I have not experienced before.

One day we use live ammunition in our rifle training. I am on my belly, my rifle resting against my shoulder with the target many meters in front. When I close my left eye as I aim, my eye trembles, distracting me from focusing with my right eye on the assigned target. I think I am the only one who cannot simply shoot. I am overwhelmed by the command to shoot, and when I do, my rifle bounces back and hits my shoulder with force. I am alarmed by the sound of the bullet leaving the rifle, and by the rifle butt hitting my shoulder. My heart is pounding. I must shoot again, they say. The next day I come prepared—my left eye is covered with a scarf. Still, I wish I were back at the barracks where I can sit in the shade under a tree.

Friday nights, after the Sabbath meal, our group of girls visits the boys of our movement, stationed in another part of the base. We go in formation. We march. As we march, we sing one of the traditional songs sung after a Friday night meal: "The Rock from Whose we have eaten! Bless Him, my faithful friends—we have eaten our fill and left over—according to Hashem's word." Some of the boys are from Jerusalem and some are from Tel Aviv. Those from Tel Aviv are of a different breed. They seem athletic and bold. We like them. We stare at them and they stare at us. We dance folk dances in circles as we hold hands.

After six weeks of basic training we are transferred for advanced training to another base, located between Jerusalem and Be'er Sheba in the south. There is something grim and gray about that base. Like the first base, it belonged to the British. For the first time, our officers are men. When my girlfriends and I want to leave the base and go home for the Sabbath, we invite our officers to share with us the delicious cookies my mother sends me. We pretend to like their company, smiling and laughing at their jokes, and we ask for a leave. On the way home we laugh and laugh about how we have succeeded in deceiving them and getting our way.

One day, as part of our training, we travel to a training area a few kilometers away from the base. When we arrive, our officer orders us to jump from the second floor of a semi-ruined house in what looks like an abandoned Arab village. I surprise myself as I jump without a thought. We hear about the Arabs' tie to the land but we don't think it is valid— the Arabs haven't sacrificed for the land, abandoning homes and families in Europe to come and till it; they haven't cultivated it and made it bloom with orchards and plants and forests. We think our claim to the land is just because it was promised to us, because we love it the way no one else does, because we have longed for it and have loved it for centuries. We loved it even before it was promised to us, in our ancient souls we loved it, even before.

On that day Ruth proves to be bold. She volunteers to stretch out on a flattened barbed-wire fence, but when we are ordered to step on her to reach the other side of the fence, we refuse. Our officer shoots his rifle in the air. At the sound of the gun we tremble, and reluctantly we rush and step on Ruth, each one of us, as she lies there still on the barbed-wire fence.

We sleep in tents, on narrow metal beds with thin mattresses. Once at night, rain seeps through our tent. Dina and I get wet and cold. We crawl into one bed and we put our suitcases over the blankets. We hope this will protect us from the rain, and though we are still getting a bit wet, we do feel protected, protected from the world, and all that is unknown to us, lying next to each other and holding each other. Sometimes, in very cold weather, we sleep on the icy floor of the cantina. Our blankets are thin and we are never warm. Often Dina suffers from a sore throat. We have no medicine, and she cannot sleep. I try to sooth her by telling her that sleep is possible. But to no avail.

We train to camouflage ourselves in an open field. I lazily roam the field and pick up thorns and leaves and stick them onto my helmet. No school or parents to fret about, only weeds to gather, and the officers barking silly-sounding orders. That night, each one of us is left alone in a field and is ordered to find the way back to the base with the help of the North Star. I am overwhelmed, standing in the open field like a scarecrow. How would I find my way back in a world that is vast and infinite, under a voluminous sky filled with luscious stars? The entire universe seems to be made up of tiny-jeweled souls. I look for the North Star, a star among so many. I am nervous. After a search I see it, blinking directly at me. I am able to figure out the direction in which I should go. Upon my return to the barracks, the base seems gloomier than before.

I am no stranger to lonely fields and roads. Once, at night, while returning to the base after visiting a friend in the hospital, I walk for miles on an empty road, passing by a bare outspread field. I am wary but unafraid. Another time I hitchhike and am picked up by a driver in a huge truck. The driver puts his arm around me. When I tell him to take his arm off me he asks how old I am. I tell him I am eighteen. He says, You are old enough. Suddenly I hear myself say, Stop right now and let me off. The words come out of me without hesitation or fear, and the voice I project is surprisingly resolute. He stops the truck immediately and lets me off. It is 11 p.m. The road is pitch dark. I don't know where I am. I walk and walk, and am surprised when I come upon what looks like a bus stop. Is it real? Indeed it is, as if planted there for my sake. I feel Grace upon me.

After a couple of months, we move to work in Kibbutz Yavneh in the south. There we live in small wooden cabins, each housing three or four people. Showers and toilets are public. Our commander has his own private cabin. We are still subject to military rules and punishments, and every morning and evening we stand in formation. During the rest of the day, I am assigned to work with a dozen children between the ages four and five. I bathe them, feed them, and put them to bed for their afternoon nap. My boss, a kibbutz woman, is lean and tall, stiff in her appearance, her black hair gathered tightly in the back. But she is relaxed and confident and her manner does not exhibit any anxiety. She tells me what to do. Still, I am at a loss about how to respond to Yehoshua, who doesn't nap, and instead puts his legs on the wall and dreams; or to Ayala, a pretty girl with dark eyes and hair, who is defiant. When a polio epidemic sweeps the country, I am quarantined, along with others on the kibbutz who work with children. I am injected with medicine, which is painful. My mother comes to visit, but is not allowed to see me.

The army routine—training, standing in formation, drills, and punishments—is meaningless. It feels more like play than a serious endeavor. There is nothing to reckon with. Our commander Michael is twenty-two years old, four years older than us. He is short and thin, with stooped shoulders and pale blue eyes. His bespectacled face looks vulnerable. He tries to establish his authority through threats and punishments. He punishes Ruth and me for giggling while standing in formation by ordering us to bring our beds and mattresses to his door in the early hours of morning. The punishment doesn't faze us.

Though Michael is a marginal character in my life, my experience with him gives me a glimpse of how trivial army life can be. To impress me with his authority, he calls me once to his office to tell me I am ordered to appear in a military court: I inadvertently violated a rule by writing to my cousin in New York and telling her where we are stationed. See what I do for you, he says without affect, tearing up the subpoena with a show of power.

Other experiences with Michael have a bizarre side to them. When Dina and I ask him for a leave to go to Tel Aviv for the day we think he will refuse. He not only agrees, but says he will join us. We are surprised. We suspect that leaving the base to spend time with us in Tel Aviv will get him in trouble with his superiors. He asks to meet outside the kibbutz near where the bus stops, to avoid being seen with us as we leave. While we wait for him at the bus stop we see him approach looking hapless, an easy target. We secretly ridicule him—his hesitant walk, the awkward way with which he carries his bag, the unsure look in his eyes. He bears none of the threatening attitude he projects as our commander back in the kibbutz. In Tel Aviv we take a walk by the beach when suddenly we are stopped by the military police, who ask for our passes. Michael assuredly pulls the passes out of his pocket. He signs them and hands them over to one of the policemen who, to our surprise, seems to have no qualms about accepting passes that are issued on the spot.

Every night Michael comes to the room that Dina, Rina, Margalit, and I share. We have a gramophone and records I brought from home. Michael knocks on the door and asks whether he can listen to music with us. He sits looking tense and barely says anything. Once, someone in our group leaves a note under his office door that says: "With Rachel, you are like the sole of a shoe." People say it is Yitzhak who left the note, and that Michael is in love with me. Yitzhak, a depressed looking guy, is an outsider who has not integrated into the group, and by some account is holding a grudge against Michael for having slighted him. The attention Michael gives me, apparent to others, has little impact on me. In spite of my aloofness, however, I feel flattered.

After a short period of time, our roommate Margalit is discharged from the army in order to marry. Margalit comes from a small town near Tel Aviv, and she is not part of our pre-army group. She was placed in our unit by chance. Although she shares quarters with Dina, Rina and I, we don't form a kinship with her. After she leaves Dina and I visit her in her new home, less out of duty or friendship, and more out of curiosity: we want to know what sexual intercourse is like. We expect Margalit to tell us titillating tales, to uncover for us the mystery of sex. We sit in her small, ill-lit room and wait. Margalit looks as she always did, with a gray expression on her face. Nothing about her has changed, and she has nothing exciting to tell us. Do you have sex with or without a night-gown? we inquire. I have it both ways, she answers, without the slightest enthusiasm.

Soon my life engenders its own romantic sparks. I meet a man named Miki in an army hospital, where we are both recuperating from the flu. Miki is from Romania, and speaks Hebrew with an accent that disturbs me. But I am impressed with his rank in the artillery corps. Miki escorts me back to the kibbutz. On the bus I want him to keep his hand on mine, to keep his body next to mine. His hand is large and warm, the touch feels strange but there is goodness in it, goodness that later, while walking on the path to Yavneh, puts me at ease: the moon leans towards us, darkness is soft, Miki puts his arms around me, he kisses me. I am flooded by a rush of an unknown excitement, and also by a feeling of security. Miki is slightly heavy, a lieutenant six years older than me, and he is genuinely fond of me. I am not in love with him, but I like him embracing me and kissing me.

In the second year of my army service our group moves to Kibbutz Be'erot Yitzhak. During the Independence War the kibbutz was forced to abandon its land near Gaza and move to its present location, further north, close to Tel Aviv. Miki's army camp is quite far from where I am stationed now, and I am flattered he comes all the way to see me in Tel Aviv. Sitting on a bench facing the sea Miki and I talk very little. But I am drawn to his body, the shape of his body, his large head, and the black army cap, all of which form an image of strength and of potency. My girlfriends ridicule his European accent. They are critical of me—they think I am loose for kissing him. But I don't care about their criticism. If they object to the relationship because he is not one of our gang, so be it!

While we, the girls, are adapting to the new kibbutz, the boys are sent to a base in the Negev for a few months of rigorous training. The girls are asked to send a letter to a boy of our choice. I choose Eitan. By now, I no longer date Miki. Eitan has blond hair, blue eyes, and a strong, sturdy body. As a native of Tel Aviv he has an air of the sea's allure and an adventurous spirit. Though I've never talked to Eitan, I write my letter with ease, and being intentionally seductive, I enclose a shower curtain ring as a hint of a future link.

When the boys return, Eitan and I begin to date. We take a hike "from sea to sea," the Mediterranean Sea to Lake Kinneret, along with Dina and her boyfriend Danny. On the tip of Rosh Hanikrah, a northern point, we pose for a picture: Eitan picks me up and carries me like one carries a bride over the threshold. One night we sleep on a concrete platform on top of a hill in Meron, which is scattered with ancient tombs. I lie next to Eitan, huddled under blankets. It is Lag B'Omer, and to celebrate it people are dancing on the platform. Eitan kisses my forehead and a glow goes through me. The next day we come upon a waterfall, a pond with glassy water. The air is damp, the sky a light-bluish spread. Eitan dives into the water. His bold, lengthy strokes radiate. I enter the water, hold onto his shoulders, and float above his body.

Once, when Eitan is sick, I visit him in the infirmary. He is alone, and very feverish. Slipping into bed with him, risking catching his illness, I feel heroic. I like feeling Eitan's strong back. I like to think of what a good swimmer he is. Eitan, who loves the sea, has been swimming there from a very early age. I imagine Eitan defiant, mastering the sea, swimming away from home, from safety, in the direction of a hazardous horizon. The sea to me, to anyone from Jerusalem, is a remote attraction, a titillating, dangerous place, where my friends and I would spend most of our time tanning on the beach, posing for pictures, or stretched out on canvas chairs. We are wary of the sea. If the waves are high and a black flag is raised, I think the sea is full of demons; when the sea is calm I feel blessed, splashing in shallow waters.

In this second year of army service, in Kibbutz Be'erot Yitzhak, we are allowed to wear civilian clothes. The girls try to keep their appearances within the simple kibbutz style. But every once in a while Dina, Rina, and I shave our legs and armpits; I put on rouge. We travel to Tel Aviv to shop for fabric, and we have the kibbutz dressmaker make us dresses that are a little fancy. In our room, furnished with three beds and a narrow closet in the wall, we hang reproductions of Renoir's woman bathing, and Van Gogh's bright-colored flowers. Once a week I go for piano lessons in Petah Tikva, a nearby town. I practice on the kibbutz piano, while Dina sits and listens. As I play, I marvel at my hands, a laborer's hands, hardened from picking melons and potatoes, and scratched from picking lemons off thorny branches. My piano teacher,

Mrs. Levy, a refugee from Yugoslavia, thinks my piano playing is on a level that merits a commitment to music, and she encourages me to pursue the study of piano as a career.

Our group develops a warm rapport with the members of the kibbutz. They greet us with a smile. When I serve them food, dressed in shorts and a white tee shirt, taking my turn in the dining room, they are especially friendly, as relaxed as their natural environment: a gentle sky, fresh-looking trees, and a light damp breeze in the evening. Many evenings, our group gathers in a large room. We sing enthusiastically the songs that have been passed on to us by the pioneers who came from Russia. But most stirring are the songs of our brigade's entertainment troupe Lehakat Hanachal (the Nachal Band). Their lyrics speak about personal yearnings, more than about the war or the nation.

Once, my mother visits me and has lunch in the dining room. She tells me later she wept on the way home, thinking the food was bad, especially the bread. That I have to eat such bread, hard, not fresh, caused her pain. I love the simple food of the kibbutz and I cannot understand why my mother wept. Did *I* mind the bread? She didn't ask. Perhaps she felt helpless. There was nothing she could do about that bread but watch me eat it.

Most of the time I work in the kibbutz fields. I get up at dawn. I like to be in the sun. I like the smell of the melon field, a smell full of promise, especially after the field has been irrigated. I like picking melons. I like holding a melon, feeling the shape of it. I like the men with whom I work, simple and straightforward. I like to prove that I can work as hard as they do.

I see Eitan working in an adjacent plot, irrigating a field. He carries pipes with deliberate movements, places them on the ground and puts them together. He is in the sun without a shirt or hat on. I revel in seeing his strong, half-naked body and blond hair. I can even sense his scent mingled with the scent of earth and water and melons. In the winter I pick oranges and put them in a sack tied around my waist. While working in the lemon orchard I climb high up on the ladder, delighting in the view of the orchard and the sheer blue sky, and bathing in the simple, unpretentious scent of lemons.

I am carefree. I am away from Jerusalem, from the anxiety that hovers over my home, a mood colored by the losses my mother and father experienced as children. In Jerusalem I must give my parents pleasure. I owe it to them to make them happy. Here in the field, or in the orchard where I pick oranges or lemons, I owe my parents nothing.

Every night I go with Eitan to his room. We undress and lie in his bed. It is a narrow bed. We don't sleep. We lie there embracing each other, stroking each other. I owe nothing to Eitan. He owes nothing to me. In summer, Eitan and I often lie on the grass outside his room. There is an afternoon breeze, and we just watch the sky, and we look at each other. Eitan has piercing blue eyes. We talk. We make no plans. We anticipate nothing, and we expect nothing.

On rainy days I work in the kitchen. All day I peel potatoes and put them in a large pot of water. I also work in the laundry as a folder, an inferior job but one with small rewards. I often come across Eitan's undergarments, which I recognize by the number inked on them, and I stealthily kiss them. I mull over what Eitan and I said and did the night before until the early hours of the morning, when I would go back to my room for a couple of hours of sleep. People in my group think Eitan and I have passionate sex. They don't know we are just eager to touch each other's nakedness, kiss and cuddle. We don't have intercourse. We don't think of marriage. We love loving each other.

9

MUSIC AND OTHER DIFFICULTIES

A change occurs after my return from the army. The Sabbath as a sacred day is losing its grip on me. I want to do away with rituals, do away with the burden and weight of observances that are forced upon me. I reject some religious rules that my parents demand I follow. I long for permission to free myself from being confined by them. Friday afternoons, my father, in a tense and anxious mood, rushes to complete the preparations for the Sabbath. His mood persists during the evening. The room where we eat is intimidating. The couch, the pictures on the wall, benign looking during the week, now have an oppressive quality. My father looks grim. My mother is expressionless. My parents want me to do *netilat yadayim*, the ritual of washing the hands before the meal. I defy them. They get angry. I wash my hands and say the blessing. I am numb to the words. My parents demand I say grace after the meal. I resist. But their displeasure is too strong for me to refuse. Once, on Rosh Hashanah, I don't get up in the morning to go to the synagogue. My father furiously stresses the obligation of attending the synagogue on this holy day. I sit up in the bed and stare at him blankly. He persists to admonish me as I resist, anchored to my bed.

The allure of an unburdened, secular life pushes aside the belief in religious commandments. My transgressions become more severe. In a car on one Sabbath Eve with my date, an architect from Tel Aviv, I feel unreal, almost as if I'm not me. We drive away from my neighborhood, alone on the road, in a car that rumbles noisily. I am committing a sin, I say to myself. My parents don't know. They are not aware of me riding away to a party, a long ways away in the southern part of the city. For the entire ride, this secret, the need to hide from them what I am doing, makes me feel at once numb and guilty.

There are writers at the party. I think of the few writers I've met before:

one, a poet introduced to me once by Eitan. She wore black from head to foot, long hair, pale face. She had an oddness about her I had not encountered before. I was intrigued by the soft way she spoke, a bit haltingly, her reticence, her white skin, her awkward slimness. Now, at the party, I dare not speak to anyone. My guilt about driving in a car on a Friday night disorients me. And anyhow, what am I doing here with these artists and writers? I study music, but I am not an artist. One of the writers speaks to me. He points to Matti Megged, a famous writer. There he is, in the flesh, sitting comfortably on a couch. I am dazzled. My guilt about profaning the Sabbath begins to fade. And for a moment, for a very brief moment, I think if I can become like one of these people, if I can become a writer, it would be doing something so inconceivable, and so wondrously strange.

I date another architect, Gavriel, who once accompanies me while shopping for a dress. The owner of Rosenblum, a high-end clothing store, approaches me while we browse there and suggests I model his clothes at the Artists' House on Friday evening. At his spacious, well-lit home that evening I try on a three-piece jersey outfit, and I descend the elegant staircase slowly, mindfully. Mr. Rosenblum and his wife praise me. They think I look professional. After the Friday night Sabbath meal, that same week, I leave my house furtively, accompanied by Gavriel. Streets are ghostly. Stores, movie houses, restaurants are closed. A car or two pass by. The Artists' House, near the King David Hotel, makes me think of soothsayings and magic, altars to Baal. In the dressing room, professional models from Tel Aviv chat and laugh loudly. I am astonished by how indifferent they are when men walk in as they undress. How different they are from us, Jerusalemites, who are modest and introverted. I undress, timidly, and put on the three-piece outfit. I shudder to hear the voice on the loudspeaker introducing me as a new model. I enter the crowded hall filled with smoke, smiling, and I open the jacket of my three-piece jersey outfit. Flood lights shine on me, live music blares. At that very moment I know I will never do this again, this empty thing, this thing devoid of meaning. For years I tell no one what I did on that Sabbath eve.

Searching to do something interesting, I apply to the Rubin Academy of Music. I play the piano for several testers, in the Tel-Or cinema hall in the center of town. I play a waltz by Chopin, and a prelude by Bach, and am accepted. I enjoy the idea of going to a prestigious school, especially when people are impressed when I tell them about it. My piano teacher is a well-known composer. The Academy is in a modern building, built with massive white stone, a courtyard as you enter, sparse and airy, and with a small pool in the middle. There is an aura about the Academy. The mood is hard to get at, somewhat esoteric. Walking in the school's corridors I hear music streaming from the classrooms, a piano, another piano, a cello; repeated phrases, striving for perfection. When the teacher talks about Gregorian chants, I envision monks within enclosed courtyards surrounded by high stone walls, singing to God. To think that the Early Middle Ages produced such singing! With all its bravura, our century is only a shadow of that splendor.

I am terrified of musical dictations. As soon as we begin an exercise I become anxious and numb. Is that an interval of a whole note, or of a half note? The teacher, a lanky, soft-spoken Frenchman, is cruel. Why else would he have us grasp at notes in the air?

I play preludes by Bach and sonatas by Mozart. I practice for two hours a day, not nearly enough to excel. I try to play correctly. But I don't feel any stirring; I don't have a sense of an internal rhythm. I use the metronome. I feel inadequate as if I have a sign on me that says, "I cannot do it." The dull furniture and the paucity of books at home, a bookcase with books such as *Do You Know Your Country?* add to this feeling. I only have a few records: *The Sabre Dance* by Khatchaturian, Schubert's *Eighth Symphony*, and swing music by Glenn Miller and Artie Shaw. I desire to have the bust of a composer on my piano. But Jewish law prohibits the owning of carved images. I tell myself, one day when I am married, living the way I please, I will buy a bust of Beethoven or Chopin and place it on my piano.

After a while, enjoying the status of studying at the Academy dies out, especially when the work becomes tedious. There is a barrier, or rather a blank, about how to proceed. In truth, the question of how to proceed does not even occur to me. I am in a deep quandary and feel aimless. I feel pain. An unfamiliar pain of being on the outside—doing something I am not fully in tune with, failing to truly absorb what I am being taught. Other students seem to be resolute, completely involved in their studies.

Sometimes after classes I visit Gad, my boyfriend. There is excitement. Delight. But there are evenings when I leave the Academy and the ambiance is elusive. Where am I to go on a night like this? The trees along the street and the plants in the private gardens are cold and distant, like contemporary music, difficult to grasp.

Alban Berg. Vozzek. Darius Milhaud. I am bewildered. But the teacher, a German Jew, a composer who, when he first came to Israel, played the piano in bars and cafés to make a living, can sing their music by looking at the score. When he sits at the piano to play, his fingers, it seems, are an extension of his ears.

I like doing my homework in Gad's room. Gad is studying to be a doctor. He is tall and has dark eyes and hair. He plays the violin and we practice Beethoven's Kreutzer Sonata. His kisses are devouring. Gad lacks tenderness, but his presence is supportive, and he helps me with my studies. Gad likes me to show him the movements I learn in a ballet class. I raise my leg above the radiator and lift my arms and bend. I know it is amateurish, but arousing.

Gad lives in a dormitory, in a building that was a convent or a monastery in the center of Jerusalem, behind Or-Gil Cinema. It is a big building with long corridors and many rooms. The stone looks ancient. The floor is made of semi-dark large square tiles. Once inside, after I shut the heavy front door and climb up a flight of stairs, the place draws me in. The walls have absorbed the spirit of enclosure.

When Gad walks me home we choose different paths on different evenings. We kiss while standing in a field or against one of the houses. I surprise myself once by putting my hands under his undershirt, feeling his skin. The first time he walked me home I was embarrassed about my dilapidated, unpaved street, the sidewalks broken in many places, the garbage cans. At my house we sit on the terrace. My grandmother, who lives with us in a room next to the terrace, moans and wails loudly, mourning the recent death of her daughter. Gad does not ask me about these sounds. And I do not tell him. We quietly stare at the houses in front, faintly lit by moonlight and stars.

When Gad's mother plans to visit him from out of town he asks, Should she bring the rabbi with her? I remain silent. Is this a marriage proposal? I thought marrying me has crossed his mind but I don't think he is serious. Would I marry him? I do not know. After a while I stop visiting Gad. We draw apart. I meet him on the street once and he asks, Why have you stopped visiting me? I have a girlfriend now who gives everything, he adds. By "everything" he means sexual intercourse.

At the Academy I am not self-contained. The music I study is undigested. Theory has no real meaning for me. Pray, pray, I think.

Pray to whom?

God is invisible. Why believe in him? Was it God who commanded the Israelites to follow the laws described in Leviticus? (Once, I had a nightmare in which God was particles in space, as if He were nothingness.) God is part of an abstract design, like the musical compositions I study.

I tell my father music school is torturous. He says, Why don't you leave?

I have marriage on my mind. Whenever I help my mother in the house I imagine myself living with a husband, tidying up my own home. The fantasy is accompanied by a cozy feeling. If I don't want to marry a man I am in love with, or think the man wouldn't marry me, I unhesitatingly break up with him. My friend Dina thinks it is highly unusual to be able to break up a relationship while feeling passionate.

It is depressing to be with men I am not attracted to. But Dina and I want "to do something," add culture to our lives. We sometimes visit with a certain group of men at one of the men's apartment. We sit on beds covered with colorful bedspreads and lean on cushions, and listen to Rachmaninoff, Beethoven, and Dvorak. One man in the group is withdrawn. One day he commits suicide, jumping from one of the buildings in the center of town. He never smiled. But who would have thought?

There is no phone in my house and the men I date often make surprise visits. Once Ya'akov visits me at home on the eve of Yom Kippur. We take a walk, and after our walk Ya'akov goes home to eat. He is oblivious about eating on a fast day. It is what his family, secular German Jews, do. For a moment I feel estranged from Ya'akov. I think eating on Yom Kippur requires, at the least, a conflict, a preliminary struggle with God.

Another time I see Ya'akov's face peering through the window of my office, situated in an inconspicuous hut behind the Ministry of Religious Affairs. I work in a department whose clandestine job is to win back children from poor Jewish families who have been lured away by Christian missionaries. Though my work is clerical, I am sent once or twice to retrieve Jewish children from the mission convents, and I find out that I have a propensity for advocacy. Ya'akov works on Israel's radio. His work is incongruous with the kind of work my office does. His sudden face in the glass makes my heart throb. I am glad to see him. Ya'akov and Gad add cheer to my life—I feel at ease, sensuous, restful. Seeing them breaks the monotony of my work and lessens the tension I experience in music school. When Ya'akov first kisses me, he points to the ground where we stand on a street and says, It is happening here, in this place, as if to commemorate the event. Most of the time Ya'akov is aloof, unattainable. Once, he says, I will marry in five years. "Five years" sounds like an unending, ungraspable span of time. Instantly, almost magically, my attachment to Ya'akov dissolves.

Counterpoint. Harmony. Acoustics. The subjects are not difficult, but they don't speak to me. I mark notes in my scores. I pass the exams. I listen to lectures about the organ, the piano clavier, and the harpsichord. There must be something out there that would truly echo in me. I think that perhaps playing chamber music in New York would do it. Or the study of a new language.

One winter when snow piles up in Jerusalem, I visit a medical student in his attic apartment with Dina and her date. We listen to the fourth symphony of Brahms. The music slowly unfolds and swells, growing from a deepish center to great heights. Rafi, our host, listens intently, looking past me and barely noticing me. His facial features are perfectly symmetrical, his body coordinated and strong. But throughout the evening he complains about turning bald. When he takes me home he talks about using massage and ointment for his baldness, to no avail. The snow rises like Brahms's music—so much is inaccessible; so much inside me remains untouched, frozen as snow.

In the summer a ticket arrives for me, from one of my mother's brothers, to sail to New York. I am on vacation from school and am happy to use it. Uncles, aunts, and cousins meet me at the port and take me to a welcoming party at my uncle's house in the city. Then I am driven to a suburb of New York. The house I stay in is large. The front yard is carefully landscaped, dotted with plants and flowers. I sleep in a room with a wall closet, a beige and green bedspread that matches the curtains and the two upholstered chairs, a light brown desk, and a couple of lamps. I indulge in a bubble bath in the large shiny bathtub, not having to worry about a water shortage. My first bath lasts for about an hour, and my cousin knocks on the door to be sure I am all right.

Saturday night is date night. I won't travel on the Sabbath, and my dates wait until night to pick me up. I sit on the front stairs of the house to watch the darkness descend and the stars appear. Three stars, and the Sabbath is over. Only then will I go out. But when it comes to dietary laws, I am more lenient. I eat the food my cousin prepares, though she is not strict with the separation of milk and meat dishes. I tell myself, This is a distant land, far away from Jerusalem, from a sacred turf. Here God is remote and transient as the clouds above Long Island's shore.

My mother's family are very generous hosts, and they show me a good time. They take me to nightclubs, museums, Central Park, popular tourist spots: the Statue of Liberty, the Empire State Building. But these places seem devoid of substance. The reality of the people, the authenticity of the streets, the truth of the architecture, escape me. The city leaves me dispassionate. Glitzy and entertaining, it remains obscure. I only touch its surface, nothing more. I don't have the curiosity to penetrate things. I wear my hair long, my dresses tight, high heels; people tell me I am beautiful. The city feels like a platform for my vanity.

Through a cousin I meet a man, Peter, a professor at a university in New York. Peter is very tall and handsome, divorced, twelve years older than I. I visit his office at the university. It has a big desk and comfortable chairs, and plaques on the wall with his name and his credentials. (A prominent New York politician consults with him and pays him $100 an hour.) Peter takes me to visit Newport, Rhode Island. The houses on the seashore rise like monuments, matching the splendor of the rocks that adorn the sea. People who live there, I think, must have grand lives. Peter persuades a restaurant owner to reopen after closing, so we can have dinner. We visit Peter's friends, who are in the movie business. Back in New York, Peter takes me to Radio City Music Hall, where we see the Rockettes, and to a movie with Ingrid Bergman whom, according to Peter, I resemble. Then he takes me to an outdoor concert in Tanglewood, where we listen to music that spreads to the farthest parts of the sprawling landscape. I am attracted to Peter. I enjoy glancing at myself from the outside, seeing how I am in the company of this successful man.

Meeting Peter opens me up to a new world, the world of psychotherapy. On a Long Island beach, Peter and I are stretched out on towels. It is hot and humid. Peter is in a bathing suit, tall and thin. How odd it is to be on this endless beach, where the sun is reticent, the people on the beach are distant, their manner of speaking, their body language, are unknowable, and Peter, though Jewish, is culturally and personally unfamiliar; no one in my past is like him. He tells me about his work. He is a sociologist and a psychotherapist. He runs groups in drama therapy. I know about therapy only vaguely, and it is the first time I hear about group therapy, drama therapy. Peter tells me how one of his patients is anxious about his penis being small. As he talks, I envision the group, and the young man standing in front of it. Something in the story, though profoundly bizarre, hits me. The young man is obviously getting help.

With Peter I experience New York differently. Every place I go with him acquires a certain charm. As soon as we enter clubs or restaurants, the Rainbow Room or a jam session, the dance floor, the tables covered with white tablecloths, the waiters smiling, the view from the window, the live piano music, cast a spell on me. Peter adds elegance to these places; perhaps it is his height, his handsome face, the ease with which he walks in, knowingly, at home. The jazz clubs, small hidden pockets of soulful music, the bass with its delicate, grave tone, the nuances and melodic phrases it produces, the black men behind it who play effortlessly, coolly, enthrall me. In one of the jazz clubs, a black man is hunched over a piano, playing as if merged with it; the bass player's manner is meditative. The jazz is uneven, surprising in parts, laden with emotional uncertainties. Peter knows some of the jazz players, he waves to them, and they smile at him. Peter is very attentive—he wants to please me. I am surprised his success and power do not make him immune to craving my love.

My mother's family in New York objects to my going out with a divorced man. They reprimand me. I feel humiliated. I think of my mother who, when living in New York, had to depend on her family's hospitality and generosity to provide her with a home. But I don't depend on anybody for a home. I can leave. I call Peter. I cannot imagine where he is, how he lives; I have never been to his apartment. I imagine him in an undefined place, with no walls or a roof, in a vacuum. I say, I am leaving America. I say it without hesitation, but I hear my voice quiver. There is silence, waves of shock. The distance between Peter and me is already widening. I experience Peter drifting away. Why are you leaving? He finally asks. I say, I've decided to go back to Israel. He says, I want to marry you, I will leave for Israel, I will learn Hebrew. I remain silent. His claims that he would go to Israel and study Hebrew don't sound real to me; more like a momentary feeling, I think. Then I say goodbye. I hadn't considered marrying him—I don't want to marry an American.

The ambiance on the Greek ship I sail on is Mediterranean, somewhat passive, submissive to fate, closer to the course of my life, like the olive tree in a field next to my house. I order kosher food, but it is unap- petizing and I switch to eating the Greek food, which is delicious. I feel guilty, but not enough to keep me from eating it. I intuit that when I tell my mother about it, she will be easy on me. She will shrug, as if to say, I wouldn't want my daughter to eat unpleasant food for two weeks. The ship's piano player has a leisurely charm, a Vittorio Gassman charm, aloof without being inattentive. His power lies in his dark good looks, his understated show of affection towards me, his courtly limp as he walks away from the piano after an evening of playing dance music. The night before the boat lands in Haifa he and I stand on the deck and look at the sea and the night and the stars. Though his face is marked with disillusionment, he seems like a Greek Cavafy character that in failure manifests courage. I feel a pause, a sense of being. Soon I will be home.

Back in Jerusalem I tell my mother I will never marry an American, nor will I live in America. Years later, my mother, distressed about my move to New York, angrily reminds me of my promise, now broken.

Sharabi Street in Jerusalem where I grew up.

Father in a
photo studio,
Jerusalem, 1925.

Mother,
Jerusalem, 1930s.

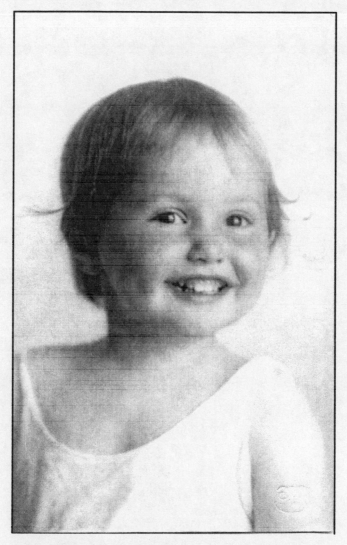

Me at age one-and-a-half.

My parents, late 1940s.

Mother and me on the
terrace of our home,
early 1950s.

Eitan and me on a hike
in northern Israel, 1954.

Proudly wearing my army
uniform, 1953.

Me (front row, third from left), in formation, 1953.

Dina in Jerusalem, late 1950s.

Mark and me, New York, early 1960s.

Me with my two boys on a visit to Israel, 1967.

Preston, 1975.

In my office, 1984.

Sara and me, 2008.

My portrait in Mark's "Legacy Project: Portraits of Artists and Writers," 2009.

10

THE SWIMMING POOL

My friend Dina is in agony. She has two boyfriends; they both love her and want to marry her. She cannot decide. She dates one, and then dates the other. What should she do? Dina and I have loyally shared our lives, knowledge, clothes, happiness, misery. I would ask my date to bring along a friend for Dina, and she would do the same for me. I tell Dina about Peter and psychotherapy. I suggest she see a therapist for consultation. But where should she go? We know no therapists, and we don't know anyone who could suggest a therapist. We decide to ask the pharmacist on Ben Yehuda Street. It is dusk, close to closing time. The pharmacist unhesitatingly gives us the name of a psychologist. On the phone the psychologist says, Come right away. We walk to his office in Rehavia, a rich neighborhood inhabited mostly by German Jews. The architecture of the houses is influenced by Bauhaus, brought over from Europe. There are a number of cafés and a tennis court; sounds of someone practicing the piano or the violin stream from the windows. Dina and I sit anxiously in the waiting room. The curtains are drawn, and only the dim light of a lamp shines in the corner. The psychologist, a short, bespectacled middle-aged man, introduces himself and invites us both in. I say, Should I come in too? Yes, yes, come in, he answers with a smile. There is a dark and heavy bookcase behind the psychologist's chair. Dina tells him about her suffering and not being able to decide whom to marry. He talks to her, and oddly enough, he talks to me too. At the end of the visit Dina pays him 15 liras. When we leave we are not sure what he said, what he advised her. But Dina has become decisive. We go to a phone booth and she calls one of her boyfriends, giving him her consent to marry.

Several months later I meet Moshe while working in the parliament as a typist. Moshe works for one of the political parties. Moshe is religious. He is smart, conceited about studying abroad, and entertaining. He is critical of some of the clothes I have bought in New York: plastic sandals, a dress with a multi-colored print. His credentials, especially his being religious, please my parents. I am in love with Moshe. We date for several months, and he asks me to marry him. I consent. I am impressed with him having studied for a year in Oxford, though what he says about James Joyce and Proust is incomprehensible to me.

Once, Moshe and I go to the woods. We lean against a rock and kiss. When we lie on the ground Moshe pulls my skirt up. When I get up I touch a slight stream of blood. Moshe gives me his handkerchief. I can't go home like this, I think. My mother will know.

After that Moshe and I make love frequently. At Moshe's parents' house when they are away. We stay at friends' homes, a hotel out of town. Our lovemaking is eager, ferocious. All that time I nudge Moshe about precautions. The thought of being pregnant is inconceivable. There would be nowhere to turn.

I read about the dancer who claps his hands and stomps his feet, unguarded. "He loses himself in the Sufi dance. The beloved does not guard her house or her window. She gives up."

At noon Moshe sometimes comes to our house from work. He has lunch, and then he and I take a nap. It is natural to accept my parents' offer that we take a nap on their twin beds. They don't seem at all concerned that Moshe and I might have sex. Though they belong to a religious community, they are not puritanical when it comes to sex, but I think they prize virginity before marriage, or they take it for granted, I'm not sure.

Moshe's mother objects to us getting married. She wants Moshe to marry a rich girl, or one whose father is an important rabbi. Moshe begins to vacillate. He won't decide on a wedding date. One day we drive along the Seven Sisters, a winding back road outside of Jerusalem, very steep, surrounded by foreboding dark-green mountains. The sun is about to set, and the mountains are layered with patches of shadows. Moshe drives fast. I put my hand on his thigh, hoping to be comforted.

My words become lumps in my chest. As the car rides downhill I wish for an accident. This will bring an end to the uncertainty, I think.

One day I go to my father's store. The often-oppressive mood at home is nonexistent at the store. The store for me is a home away from home. There is comfort in the lively, business-like atmosphere. Both my parents are in the store. I go behind the wall of shelves, in the back of the store, weeping. My sobbing is sudden; I am unaware of wanting to share my pain with my parents. I've lost twenty pounds. I think I will never find a man to marry. The only thing I say to my parents is that I broke my engagement. My parents look sorrowful. They don't ask me to explain anything. They don't try to comfort me, and they don't give me advice. Their presence is tender and strong. They are beside me. My heart breaks for them. I have caused them pain. They have already bought an apartment for my fiancé and me; my mother has already prepared towels and sheets, which lie neatly in her cupboard.

I weep alone at home, and often in the company of Eitan, who has remained my friend. I am grateful to Eitan for holding my hand when I call Moshe and tell him I will not see him anymore. I visit Eitan almost every night for a month in the dormitory of the university where he resides. I always find him in his room studying. He interrupts his work to be with me. He doesn't say much. He just holds me. With my head on his chest I weep, and he is able to comfort me.

A year later I notice a newcomer at the swimming pool of the President Hotel, which I visit daily. The first time I see the newcomer at the pool is when I come out of the water and find myself facing him. He is sitting on a beach chair reading a thick, black hardcover book. His body, lean and tan, the head slightly bent in a focused manner, draws my attention. When he looks up I notice his blue pupils glistening. Who are these people? I ask the friend who accompanies me that day, pointing at the man and the friend with whom he is sitting. My friend doesn't know. It is clear they aren't Jerusalemites, nor are they Israelis. The tan, lean man is a complete stranger who has landed on my tiny horizon from nowhere, resonating a mysterious destiny. Is it the shine in his eyes that attracts me, a sensuousness I had not sensed in any of the men

I had dated? I discover later that the chlorine in the water caused the sparkle in his eyes.

I have a job as the Hebrew secretary of the editor of the English language *The Jerusalem Post.* As a bonus, the employees receive free tickets to the swimming pool. Like most Jerusalemites I am a poor swimmer; I am still learning how to swim. Every time I am there I see the lean and tan man accompanied by the same friend. The man notices me too; especially on the day I am caring for my seven-year-old cousin. Later, I learn that he liked the unlimited patience with which I treated her. The friend who accompanies him was forever pointing out possible flings and when he pointed me out, the man said, No, I'd only be interested in her if I wanted to get married.

One day this newcomer and I bump into each other on the way out of the President Hotel. Would you like a lift into the center of town? He asks. Yes, I say. In the car I meet another of his friends. They introduce themselves as Americans. My name is Mark, the man says, I am from Buffalo. I know Buffalo is an animal, but a city? The friend, Albert, a big and husky man, a bit disheveled, sits in the back of the Deux Chevaux. He is from New York. As I close the door of the car the metal door feels so flimsy I think it will bend. Mark asks me if I want to have coffee with him, I say, Yes. And could he pick me up that evening to go to a jam session. A jam session? What's that? Jazz, he says. Oh, yes, I want to go. I work shifts at the paper, I tell him. Could he pick me up at the office after my afternoon shift? Yes.

Mark visits me frequently at home. He doesn't seem to mind the dilapidated street or the small quarters of our apartment. The dining room on the right of the narrow corridor has a table with four chairs, a refrigerator, and a bed on which my grandmother, my father's mother, sleeps. On the wall there is a painting of pink roses in a vase. On the left of the corridor are a small kitchen and a bathroom, and at the end is the living room, which has a coffee table, two easy chairs, a small bookcase, a piano, and a couch on which I sleep. On the wall there is a painting of sheep grazing in the meadow, which my parents bought on the recommendation of their friends, the Horowitzes, owners of a small grocery store a few streets away. To the right of the living room is my parents' bedroom, where I often do my homework on a desk that was put there especially for this purpose.

My mother welcomes Mark with a hearty smile and usually makes him something to eat. She is happy to chat with him in her American-accented English. By this time, her attitude has changed. She doesn't seem to mind that almost all my boyfriends, except for Moshe, who became my fiancé, are secular. She is friendly and warm towards them, she serves them food and drink, and sometimes she stays in the living room to chat. She does not inquire about where and how I spend my time with them. She says she trusts me. My father sits in his chair in the dining room facing the corridor. He is quiet most of the time. (Language, perhaps, cannot express the frightful conditions under which he grew up, and the frightful things he has seen.) When one of my boyfriends goes by, he lifts his eyes, then lowers them. His eyes are very expressive, but I cannot tell whether the expression is that of bewilderment, or of resignation to the inevitability of it all. I am sharing my life with him, but the sharing is wordless. Though my father rarely speaks to my boyfriends, or remarks about them, I know he has his opinions. (It never occurs to me to ask him what he thinks or what he feels.) On one rare occasion he remarks that he would like me to think of Haim, a suitor, as a potential man to marry. He knows the family, a solid well-to-do clan who trades in leather. He thinks they are a good family, and the young man is very nice and a suitable match for me. But my father's suggestion falls on deaf ears.

On many days when I work the morning shift at the paper, Mark and I meet for breakfast at Café Alaska on Jaffa Road. We eat croissants with butter and jam and have coffee. I imagine the people around us who look absorbed in their thinking to be writers and artists, living freely. For lunch we sometimes meet at Café Atara on Ben Yehuda Street, and have grilled cheese sandwiches. I love these meals with Mark. Mark talks about psychoanalysis, and movies by Godard and Buñuel. I envision the scenes from his vivid descriptions. I become part of his world—his art, his analysis—the insecure, daring, ambivalent, curious world he embodies. It is Mark's artistic sensibility, his being an artist, his otherness, his singularity, which I find so attractive and which I desire.

After we date for ten weeks, Mark leaves for Paris. We correspond. In one of my letters I say, You give me life, you are the arriviste who showed me unknown places, a neighborhood in a valley where one can almost hear a heavenly sound roll from the Judea mountains. You took me, I write, to a small house made of rough stone, which belonged to a Yemenite woman. There you bought me a big silver ring with a red bead, and a Yemenite outfit, black pants and a shirt, embroidered at the hem and around the collar with reds and greens. Above the valley, at a breezy time of the day, we walked to the monastery of John in the Wilderness, a monastery strapped to a mountain, built of stone, the color of earth, pink and brown.

Every day I wait for the mailman, and as soon as I see him from the terrace of our apartment, I rush down. It is April and the almond trees burst with whiteness as on the third day of creation. I read Mark's letters when I am alone. Sometimes I wait until night, when I am outside the house, going somewhere. I want to be alone with his letter, and I might read it under a street lamp. I read it over and over again. Mark proposes. He wants to marry me. I don't know whether I want to marry him. He says if I will marry him he will come back to Jerusalem; if I don't he will go back to New York.

I am sick with the flu. I have a high fever. I cannot go to the seaport in Haifa to meet Mark. Mark decides to come back to Jerusalem in spite of my hesitations. He enters my house wearing a brown suede jacket. He looks hesitant, vulnerable around the mouth and chin. He is holding a record, Schubert's "The Trout," a gift for me. He wants to know how I am. I say I am fine. But I am weak. I can't get up to greet him. His friend who went to meet him at the seaport had already told him I was sick. Mark tells me his voyage on the boat from France was fine. He puts the record on the record player and we listen. The piano sparkles, the cello sings, the trout darts back and forth, the river shimmers.

During the summer I anguish. One morning I wake up and I can't get up. The room is spinning. I vomit. My mother calls the doctor. He takes a urine sample. They must think I am pregnant. Everything spins. Mark says, After we get married we will move to New York for two years. I say, That will be awful, to leave my parents, leave my country. The room spins. I vomit. It is safer to lie in bed, keep warm and secure, without moving.

One day, in September, of that year, a few months after Mark's return to Jerusalem, my father seats me at the dining room table, and says, What is going on with you and Mark? If I don't marry Mark, I say, I will be miserable for the rest of my life. It doesn't take long—my father bangs on the table with his right hand and says, So marry him. I say, But I will be moving to America. My father, in a tone of resignation, says, A woman should follow her husband wherever he goes; it says so in the Bible.

Though Moshe and I were attracted to each other, though I desired Moshe and he desired me, the desire lacked tenderness. It lacked a meaningful commitment. But it paved the way for me to marry Mark. Even though I might move to America, even though Mark is not religious, my parents wouldn't stop me now (even though my mother reminds me that when I returned from visiting New York, I said I will never marry an American). Not now, after the disappointment they and I suffered. I feel I can pursue what I deeply want, to marry Mark.

I make plans to move to New York. I am distressed about leaving the land I was taught never to leave. Nevertheless, when an old friend tells me I am a traitor, I feel the comment is gratuitous. Until now it has never occurred to me to live outside Jerusalem. Whenever I leave, even for a short time, I miss the intimacy of Jerusalem, its soul, the Divine Presence at sunset before the Sabbath.

Sometime before the wedding I go to the Mikvah, prescribed by Jewish law for the purpose of achieving ritual purity, as a condition to be married by a rabbi. Before immersing myself, the *banlanit* washes me under a shower and cuts my nails. Her look is severe, her speech strict, and suddenly I am struck by terror that she might, by some intuition or by a manual examination, discover I am not a virgin. My body tightens, cringes. I think she must know. She is talking to me in an abrupt kind of way. She will expose me as a fraud. My mother will know. There will be a scandal. Something I could never live down. After the shower, I immerse myself in the water of the Mikvah. When I lift my head from under the water I see my mother weeping. She smiles at me. She looks happy. Her soft weeping is contrary to the terror I feel, and it annoys me. In moments like these my mother and I could bridge the gap between us — if only she could be less angry with me, and I could appreciate her wisdom.

A seamstress makes me a short, white satin two-piece wedding dress. My friend Hannah, who makes beautiful jewelry, makes me a silver wedding ring. I want nothing too traditional. Everything should be understated. Even the hall where we get married is simple. At the wedding I am overwhelmed, feeling numb. I greet my friends and my co-workers, but I don't feel present. I am not able to feel my excitement. The conflict about marrying Mark dissolves, but there is an anxiety about moving away to New York, the city my mother emigrated from years before. I will return to the land of her upbringing, to live in unfamiliar territory, as if predetermined to do so.

For our honeymoon Mark and I go to a hotel on Lake Kinneret. We visit Safed, graves of sages, the border with Lebanon. We visit Kefar Nahum, where Jesus embarked on a boat with his disciples. Every night, when we go to the dining room of the hotel, I try to look my best, for Mark's sake. I wear either my green velvet dress or my tight-fitting black dress, which my seamstress made for the occasion. I put on the high-heeled black shoes that Mark sent me from Italy on his way to Paris. In Kefar Nahum a priest that cups my husband's hands and mine, a drunken priest who, upon hearing that we just got married, mumbles a blessing that we will have a son. At night, I wear one of my five baby-doll pajamas that I brought back from New York a few years before, each in a different color. And every afternoon I call my mother at my father's store. I dutifully tell her I am doing fine.

Mark and I move into the apartment in Jerusalem my parents bought for my former fiancé and me. Mark uses a pint-size room as his studio. He paints abstract. He has his first one-man show in a Jerusalem gallery.

We plan to move to New York four months later, in May. I am beginning to shed religious practice. On Friday nights, when we go to my parents' house, we ride our Vespa halfway to their house. During the week, on a few occasions, I eat in one of the few non-kosher restaurants in the city. It is a change that occurs gradually, naturally. I no longer want to be subjected to rules I have not chosen to follow. In the past, I would, on rare occasions, do the same, but those were momentary aberrations. Now, I am married; I have my own home; I have my own man; I make our bed, something I dreamed of every time I made my parents' bed. I am making a life out of my own will. I have moved away from my mother monitoring me. I slowly leave the practice of religion, but the subject remains a trigger for my fear and guilt. I continue to work as a secretary at the newspaper. At home I try to be a good housewife. I teach myself how to cook—mashed potatoes, sautéed mushrooms, carrot salad. I clean the house: bathrooms, floors. I dust the furniture. I prepare a small dinner for a few friends that takes many anxious hours.

On the ship from Israel to France, on our way to New York, I realize I am pregnant. I have no appetite. In Paris, I am only able to digest croissants and cream cheese. We go to the Riviera, and we stop at an inn in Antibes. We have lunch in a small garden shaded by a grapevine. The table is covered with a red-checkered tablecloth and we are served red wine. Our room has green wooden shutters and rays of sun streak through in the morning. The ambiance is intimate, secluded, private. I am away from my discordant life. Behind trees, shrubs, and the grapevine, I am in accord with everything. On the beach in Saint Tropez, the women lie bare-breasted in the sun. Wearing a bikini, I yield to the sun, offering my body to its brilliant light. I lie there, on the sand, half-conscious, thought-free. Nothing comes to mind. At night Mark applies vinegar to my burned skin. Then in London, I take a test. I am pregnant. Mark and I cancel our reservation on a boat, S.S. Rotterdam, to New York. We decide, instead, to fly.

PART II

GIVING BIRTH

My husband and I live on 199th Street in Manhattan, near the
elevated subway. We hear the subway, a long, big, rolling sound of
unrest. I am in my third month of pregnancy with our first child, and
am tired most of the time. The door to our building has no locks, there is
no doorman, nor is there a buzzer. We have rented the apartment with
furniture; it has a massive ugly couch and a coffee table from the thirties,
blond wood and brown upholstery, a large mirror in the bedroom and a
large, cumbersome bed.

Mark and I make demands on each other. Mark becomes enraged. I
am temperamental. But we are friends. We like each other and I like to
please him. For his birthday I buy him a gadget with which he is able to
stretch his canvasses. His interests are different from those of my friends
or the men I dated. As in the past, he likes to tell me about avant-garde
movies and psychoanalysis. The movies he likes are visually impacting,
ferociously imaginative, with bizarre plots. After we see *Viridiana* by
Buñuel we quarrel. He thinks it is good and original. I think it is a bit
pretentious. But I begin to cultivate a taste for these movies. Later, I am
entranced by Fellini's *Roma*, the depiction of brothels in Rome, whores
with heavily painted faces parading their graceless bodies, and a madam
who sends the men away by spraying them with insecticide, using the
kind of a hand pump we used to kill flies in Jerusalem. I ask myself
whether my affinity for Italian and Spanish films has to do with having
lived in proximity to the Mediterranean Sea, and in a landscape similar
to theirs—rugged hills, dry fields, olive trees—sharing a background that
includes a struggle with and a thirst for God. Perhaps it is presumptuous
to think I have a commonality with Buñuel and Fellini, or with Italian
authors such as Natalia Ginsberg and Calvino, whom I discover on my
own, and who are very appealing to me.

Mark also introduces me to the lonely beat of the jazz music of Miles Davis and Charlie Parker, Billie Holiday and Sarah Vaughan, who are at once close to the course of life and otherworldly. I admire the capacity of these musicians to improvise, a capacity I think I do not possess. The blues reach deeper in me; they feel closer to Jewish sacred music, the *Hallel*, for instance, sung by Yoselah Rosenblatt: "From the straits did I call upon God, God answered me with expansiveness."

While still pregnant Mark and I move to the Upper West Side of Manhattan. Mark sculpts and paints in the apartment. He sculpts in wood, drinking many cups of coffee a day. The noise of his saw as he cuts wood is jarring. But I accept it. The figures he makes are sharp-edged. The faces lack expression. Perhaps he wants to give them an impersonal look; perhaps they represent New York. I try to help Mark get an exhibition of his work; I visit galleries and show art dealers slides of his work. I dress up for these occasions. In the winter I put on a green suede coat and a green suede hat. From the way gallery owners look at me I know I look attractive. One well-known gallery owner comes to the house to see Mark's work. Mark sees his interest in his work as an achievement.

I work at the Jewish Theological Seminary on 120th Street, near Harlem, as a typist in English and Hebrew. Harlem fascinates me, perhaps because my mother lived there. I look at a photograph of my mother as a child, wearing a white dress, a large white ribbon in her hair, and short brown boots. She stands next to her younger brother, leaning on him, with a big smile. This was when they lived in Harlem; when she accepted life, as she always would, compromising, wanting to please, ready to fulfill some domestic task. I ride the subway my mother rode, and go to the movie theaters she went to. I visit her brothers and sisters-in-laws, nieces and nephews. I am a link between my mother and her family, an emissary. My mother wants me to see more of her family, but she prefers to live where she is, in Jerusalem, at a distance.

Lunchtime, I go to the lounge next to the bathroom, where a group of young black women employees meet every day, and I lie on the couch and doze off. My pregnancy tires me. As if in a dream I hear them talking and laughing. I feel close to these women, their realness is comforting.

When I am in labor my husband takes me to the hospital, which is in an old building in upper Manhattan. He is not allowed to be with me. I pace the floor and breathe the Lamaze way to ease the pain. The rooms in the hospital are large, with very high ceilings. The walls and floors are painted brown. I have been in labor now for almost thirty hours. I explain to a nurse that I am breathing according to the way I was taught, expecting to have natural childbirth, but she ignores me. At some point she directs me to a bed that is more like a large crib, and tells me that I have been in labor for too long and that they will induce birth.

Water flows out of me, and suddenly excruciating pains. The image of a watermelon trying to come out of me flashes through my mind. I hear women screaming. I decide to scream too. I hear myself calling my mother. Then, without any warning, they give me anesthesia.

I wake up in a large, semi-dark room. I am told that my doctor left for a vacation. While pregnant, I saw him every month. I told him about my Lamaze classes and discussed with him my desire to have natural childbirth. He said, Yes, you will have natural childbirth. It didn't occur to me that he, as it turned out, would not go along with my wishes, and that the nurses would not collaborate with me. It didn't occur to me before giving birth, that in a waiting room by myself, I would be lonely. I was too preoccupied with the prospect of having a baby to know, and least of all to expect, what I wanted others to do for me. I don't claim my right to be angry with the doctor for deceiving me, for not being present in the delivery room before or after I had anesthesia, and for not giving me a chance to talk to him and to protest. I accept things the way they are, the way they turn out to be. I am new in the country. And though I have my husband, family, and friends, I feel alone.

In my hospital room the windows are wide and long, facing a pale sky. A nurse brings my baby to me for the first time, a chubby and puffy little boy. I hold him. The nurse pushes my breast into his mouth. This is how you breastfeed, she says. When she leaves, I burst into tears. A faint light streams through the windows. The walls echo a wooden silence. Two rows of beds lined up against the walls are empty. My baby breastfeeds. Energy is drained out of me. There is no other life.

At home a nurse, a Jewish woman, warm and friendly, helps me take care of the baby. I am afraid giving my baby a bath and she says, You can do it. She stands by me and reassures me. On the day she leaves, on her way to the door, I am sitting on a chair in the hall. I put my arms around her, my head into her body. I sob. I ask her not to leave. She smiles good-heartedly and says, You'll do all right.

From an early age I envied men. I envied their freedom to be active in the world and be engulfed by their work. But there has always been the domestic pull, life indoors, the ease with which I wait and listen, the security that comes along with making a bed, setting a table.

I enjoy avocado and beer for lunch. I curl up on the couch and feed my baby. He naps. I nap. When he is eight months old I buy him a swing and hang it from the doorframe. One day he falls off the swing. I call the doctor and he says to make sure he does not fall asleep. I lie next to him. I am vigilant.

My baby loves to eat, he loves to bathe, and he loves to play. He is content. His belly laugh resonates deep in me. Whenever I bathe him or dress him I sing to him, or I talk to him, and we smile at each other. My every particle cares for him.

Even when my body is sleepless, I feel attuned to my baby. But when my baby cries after a feed, I become anxious. I am convinced my milk is too thin, weak, not nourishing enough. Am I holding back, protecting my body from being drained? Or perhaps I am too intent, impeding the natural flow of milk. Other mothers seem to be at ease while breast-feeding. I feel my milk is unwholesome; the experience of the poet Rivka Miriam resonates with me,

> Never will I be like the mother in the picture
> suckling a baby from a white breast . . .
> My children will suckle from me the ash[1]

My husband is a zealous advocate of breastfeeding and he monitors me. But I begin very quickly to supplement the feed with a bottle. When my baby still cries, my husband rushes to enlarge the hole in the nipple of the bottle.

Sometimes I lie on the couch and stare at the ceiling, unable to get up. I am depressed. I am in a kind of a shock. In this foreign country everything is different. People are separated, sometimes isolated. I get up in the morning, thousands of miles away from my native city, and ask myself, What am I doing here in a strange country, not speaking my native tongue? I look in my address book to find someone to call, to be in touch.

In summer I take my baby to Jerusalem for a two-month visit. My parents meet us at the airport. I hand my baby over to them and rush back to pick up my suitcases. My father tells me that when I handed the baby to him it was a moment of great joy, a moment of wordless trust and linkage that will be engraved in his mind for the rest of his life.

My friend Dina brings a playpen, a stroller, and diapers. My baby sleeps in the crib I slept in as a baby. Mornings, I nestle in a "comfort chair" on the terrace while my baby plays in his playpen. The terrace, suspended between a demanding outside world and the domestic routine of everyday, is unchallenged by the vicissitudes of life. The terrace is where on Sabbath afternoons my parents settle in leisurely, cracking pumpkin seeds, chatting with the neighbors. Because of its southern exposure, they particularly enjoy it in cool autumn or chilly spring, warming themselves up after eating *cholent* in the cold dining room.

I like taking walks and visiting familiar buildings. One day, I leave my parents' house in the morning and go to the neighborhood where my high school is. The building and the courtyard have not changed. I think of how, in the past, I never looked closely at the building, its windows and its courtyard. I look up at the window on the second floor where I sat by a window at a long desk with two classmates. The window, narrow and rectangular, plain and worn, with a faded green frame, was a steadfast witness imbued with an unflappable truth, a mute companion of the wonder, fear, and defiance I experienced in classes. I was often distracted. I didn't participate in class for fear of sounding stupid, my mind felt empty when the teacher asked a question, and when on rare occasions I raised my hand, I blushed and felt embarrassed to hear my voice. I was surprised when a teacher once said my answer was intelligent. I had no political or intellectual opinions, and other people who had strong convictions and the confidence to express them impressed me.

The window was also a witness for the love I felt for the opening chapter in Genesis in which the earth produces plants and trees; there is no death yet, or war, or disease, and the trees bear fruit and the plants bear seeds. There are several kinds of trees that God created through the power of his word, and every kind of living creature that lives in water. And God saw it was good. At the time I read these chapters I could see the trees and the plants, and I thought of Jerusalem still lacking in trees, plants, water.

I remember the teacher discussing Balak—a character in my beloved Agnon's *Only Yesterday*—a stray dog whose skin was lettered in jest with the words "mad dog" by Isaac, a house painter, the anti-hero of the novel. The dog, unaware of the reason for being chased, runs in the streets of Jerusalem—Meah Shearim or Nachalat Shiva, streets I know intimately—to escape the people who persecute him. He is, like Isaac, a captive of his fate. I wanted to stop Balak from running amok, and I was relieved when he stopped and sat under a tree. And Isaac, poor Isaac, I wanted to reverse his steps—I hoped against all hope that the next time he met Sonia, the woman he loved, he would be less awkward, less submissive; he would revolt against his destiny and capture her heart. For all my embarrassment for Isaac, I felt enriched by the story, by the courage of its author not to shrink from fully depicting such an unfortunate character.

The atmosphere in my parents' home is hospitable, and the meals are sumptuous. My boy responds happily to my parents' loving attention. I enjoy my parents' care, the neighbors' friendliness, the morning sun warming up the street, the sky at night rich with stars. But there is also tension. I am disappointed in myself for not being openly defiant when my mother asks me about my religious practice. I resent her grievances about me not writing to her enough when I am in New York. I gladly make the yearly pilgrimages to Jerusalem, but would be infinitely grateful if she didn't expect it. I don't feel an inner freedom I long for, the permission to say, No, I need to do what I want, come and go as I wish. My voice is dormant. I am Agnon's Isaac, restricted from revolting openly, from fully expressing my truths.

Back in New York the apartment is dark; the electricity burns all day. I miss the light in Jerusalem, the white walls and floors of my parents' home, the terrace open to a southern sun in the afternoon. I don't feel close to this city. I settle into a life with little familiarity. Shopkeepers seem to be role-playing, unlike shopkeepers in Jerusalem whose faces are genuinely friendly or express suffering. There is no particular smell to the shops. The movie theaters lack the tenderness of my hometown movie houses. Museums do not enjoy the intimacy of the only museum in Jerusalem with its modest sculpture at the entrance and the flower garden perked up by red chrysanthemums. Forty-second Street and its neon lights are a blur. As I look at the smiling faces on billboards across huge buildings I become nostalgic, even for the petty notices put up by zealots in Jerusalem admonishing people for their irreligious acts, mainly women for wearing immodest clothes. I remember Freya and Rubin, the homeless "crazy" couple. Rubin had a beard, his pants baggy, his shirt crumpled. Freya wore a wide skirt and an oversized shirt and shoes that were too big for her, and her hair was unwashed. Rubin and Freya were cheerful and talkative, though they spat at or cursed those who ridiculed them.

But it is a relief to be anonymous; to have this desired privacy in New York. After a while I begin to revel in my new freedom as a stranger in this city—away from my overbearing home, and my restrictive, confining city—to come and go without being watched, to speak without being monitored, to feel my feelings. Summers, I walk with shorts on, no one judges me. But guilt about having left is a constant, heavy burden.

When my boy is a year-and-a-half I become pregnant again. I enjoy this pregnancy. I feel alive. I buy maternity clothes at Lord and Taylor. I have a new obstetrician who says he will support my having natural childbirth.

Mark and I quarrel. He decides to see Preston McLean, his former psychoanalyst. After seeing him he tells me that Preston wants to see me. I cry. I cry for two days. Why does he want to see me?

For my first session with Preston I dress up—a cotton navy pregnancy dress, a turquoise turban and long silver earrings. Preston and I sit on chairs opposite each other. Preston is homely, big ears, odd-shaped nose, stooped shoulders. Yet there is something attractive about him. I immediately trust him. I burst into tears and say, I feel guilty about leaving Israel, leaving my mother. Preston peers at me from behind his glasses. Why do you feel guilty? he says. Your mother sent you here so you can send her pleasure back like a shooting star. I feel held. An absorbing guilt lifts.

Out on the street I grow wings. I imagine a lover. I see myself sitting on a chair, silently baring my breasts. And I envision a tree, a little girl peeling off the bark, weeping over her lost ribbon. On my lover's chair I see myself loosening my hair. I stroke his hand. The little girl's mother is strewing the ribbon with ashes, strewing it with green ashes. On the chair I unravel my colors. I bind the lover with red.

My next session with Preston takes place five weeks later, after he comes back from his summer vacation, and after I give birth to my second child. Preston invites me to visit a seminar he teaches on the interior life. I tell him the reading for seminar will take too much time away from my being a parent. He says, If at the age of eighteen one of your children dies in a plane crash, you will have the interior life. I am frightened by the remark; shocked that Preston would utter such an anathema. I don't believe that anything could replace the loss of a child. But I am attracted to the idea of having something that is my own, a self that is alive.

The following week I am on my way to the seminar, for which I have been reading G. E. Moore's *Principia Ethica*. It is spring. The trees in

Central Park bloom with a poignant beauty. I feel close to Moore's common sense philosophy, and I experience my mind expanding in different directions, a burst of thoughts I have not experienced before. In an imagined dialogue with Moore I tell him that he fails to make a distinction between pleasure and happiness. The realization shocks me into a sudden, throbbing headache. Preston is impressed by my insight.

Preston's office, where the seminar takes place, has Tibetan tangkas hanging on the wall depicting the Boddhisatva warding off wrathful deities and abiding with peaceful ones. On a small table there is a Tibetan bell used to expel demons. The seminar—The Interior Life Seminar—is interdisciplinary. It involves reading source material from the great religions and philosophy, and readings from psychology, poetry, and biology, and explicating the logic and method of commitment. Discussions involve applying notions to everyday life. Preston prompts the students to think for themselves; to feel free to understand the material in their own way; to discover what is meaningful to them in a visceral, intellectual, emotional way. In the seminar I speak spontaneously without fearing censorship, retribution, or disagreement.

My experiences in religion have consisted of following Jewish law and ritual, Jewish prayers, the study of the Bible, Mishna and Talmud, with the goal of preserving the Jewish tradition. The differences in methods, purposes, and goals in other religions strike me: the sacred, glorious ceremonies of Confucius that stress the great relationships of filial piety; the elemental, uplifting Zoroastrian prayers that distinguish clearly between good and evil: "I praise good thoughts, good words, and good deeds and those that are to be thought, spoken, and done. . . . I do renounce all evil thoughts, evil words, and evil deeds."[2]

Almost everything I read for the seminar speaks to me. Tu Fu, the 8th century Chinese poet, began to write poetry after being greatly disappointed about not having received the official position he desired. Preston remarks that as readers we benefit from this unfortunate turn of events: Tu Fu's poems are exquisite in their expression of tender love and the heartbreaking sadness of separation from family for long periods of time. As I read the poems I weep. Why is my weeping so heartfelt, so deep? Does the separation from my parents, my city and friends, move me to such wrenching sadness? Or is the weeping a premonition of something to come, a glimpse into the future: "I am living a stolen life in the evening of age; Even homecoming means but little peace and joy. The dear boy keeps close to my knees; He fears that I might again go away. . . . As I think over our needs, I have at least a hundred worries. Thank God, the harvest has been good; And I can almost see the drippings from the wine press. At least there will be enough to drink, To assuage the memories of frustration."[3]

Tearfully I read Dietrich Bonhoeffer's *Letters and Papers from Prison* to his parents. (Bonhoeffer, the German Christian minister and scholar, was imprisoned by The Third Reich for resisting Nazism.) Bonhoeffer's faith, coupled with his great sense of gratitude, helps him redeem his separation from his family by summoning them in his head. In a letter to them he says, "When the bells rang this morning, I longed to go to church, but instead I did as John did on the island of Patmos, and had such a splendid service of my own, that I did not feel lonely at all, for you were all with me, every one of you."[4]

Preston's comments on the reading material he assigns are original, "like sparks coming out of his head" as a psychiatrist, a student of his, says to me. Preston speaks with authority. He never says the same thing twice. He makes accessible the lives of great religious and spiritual personalities. I am porous. I absorb his ideas. On a couple of occasions I weep when I hear a new idea. Something in me is born: my intellect, my creativity, dormant in all those years I lived in Jerusalem. Preston gives precise feedback to what a student says, a response that seems to issue from intuition and a depth of knowledge. In a flash of ingenuity he remarks that Buddha's omniscience, his ability to read people's minds, is a reward from his conscience for being true to his vows. The idea fills me with wonder, the kind of wonder a child feels coming upon a blossoming tree in spring, or seeing the ocean for the first time.

12

AWAKENING

Labor pains creep up on me as I watch a Hitchcock movie. I sweat profusely, and I tell the friend who is with me that I am about to give birth. He says, Let's watch the second movie and then we will go. But I need to go now. We take a taxi home and my husband rushes me to the hospital. The nurse has no time to shave my pubic hair, and she is hardly able to give me an enema. I am wheeled to the delivery room. Pains increase. My doctor walks next to me. Do you still want to have natural childbirth? he asks. I say, No, no.

I wake up from anesthesia. Was I dead? I see images from the Hitchcock movie. The doctor says I have a boy. I bleed heavily. They wheel me to the intensive care unit. My husband is sitting next to me. Will I die? I ask. No, he says. The nurse says, Don't worry, we are in touch with the doctor every hour.

When the bleeding stops I am moved to a private room. I realize that this doctor has also deceived me. Asking me whether I want natural childbirth in a moment of intense pain was meant to discourage me from having natural childbirth.

From the window I see the lights of Manhattan, colorful neon, blinking. My uterus contracts. They bring my baby. I hold him. He is lean and long. When he breastfeeds my uterus contracts with more intensity, having a life of its own.

It is 95 degrees in our apartment. We have a fan but it does very little to alleviate the heat. My husband goes sailing, leaving me with a nurse and my mother-in-law. My head throbs. I breastfeed my baby while my two-and-a-half-year old circles around me, puzzled.

While sitting on the steps of a brownstone next to my building one day I burst out crying. If I go inside I will not be able to leave. I am overwhelmed by having two children.

During a three-month period of breastfeeding my older son, I thought I didn't have enough milk. After only two weeks of breastfeeding my younger son, I once more think I don't have enough milk. I often feel I am not good enough. My wanting to be perfect interferes with the feeling that I am good enough. My mother acknowledges that she wants me to be perfect. If I had had many children, she says, and one of them turned up with faults, I could always have looked at the others and have said, They have what this child doesn't have. But in our family you are the only one.

Our pediatrician says that giving a baby a bottle is just as good as breastfeeding. I believe what I hear and read. I think theorists know what is best. I have not yet learned that there is beauty in waiting for the baby to find the breast; that my baby crying does not reflect my failure to breastfeed. I want to do the right thing. Fashion is the venue for doing the right thing. Breastfeeding is not in fashion. I stop breastfeeding and give my baby a bottle. I hold him close. My baby has a penetrating, intelligent look. He likes me to sing to him. I sing a Hebrew song, over and over again, about a bonfire and people sitting around it.

In my poem "Simplicity" I tell my son to listen to the muses rather than recite his math. I want to be myself. I want to read Brazilian poems on the streets and wail aloud over Gabriela Mistral's aching words. I want to knock on the door of a beloved and ask if I can come into his bed and pull the sheet over our bodies.

I meet mothers in the playground, and I learn new things from them: where to buy children's clothes, the use and value of paper towels, brand names for floor polish and laundry powder, the differences between them. I also learn new recipes for making steaks, roast beef, stews, and chicken. I use a heavy cast-iron frying pan with ridges, which my husband insists is the best pan for steaks. When our children are older the other mothers and I form a playgroup for them. Once a week I have a free day.

Sometimes my husband and I and our two boys go to a Hungarian restaurant on Broadway that serves *palacinka* (crepes). The pace is slow. Flavored scents stream from the kitchen. We are served cucumbers with vinegar, then a goulash, and the palacinka comes last. While we wait for each course the kids become impatient, they throw things; it is good that no one minds. The people in the restaurant are patient. I have a faint sense of living in a community.

I feel a mixture of love and anxiety towards my boys. I am conscious of feeling cruel when I once asked my older boy how his day was in school, knowing he hates the question. I sometimes feel a small power in taunting him, ridding myself of and projecting my own anxiety about his well-being onto him. I want every bit of happiness for my boys. I imagine I can deliver happiness to them. I sometimes omit looking under the surface, under the happiness and the unhappiness that appears to be there, or that I imagine being there. Sometimes I think I have been driven by ideas about how they ought to be, how well they ought to do, ideas that come from the culture I have not consciously adopted. I love my boys deeply, I listen to what they want, I want to give them what they want. I listen to them about how they feel, and I imagine what they feel, and sometimes I find out I am mistaken. I sing to them at night while putting them to bed. Once my younger boy has hives and I hold him on my lap for an hour and see his hives gradually vanish. Another time when I stand next to his crib and he is crying, I am so overwhelmed by his crying I become numb, standing there not moving, not picking him up.

My older boy likes to go on the subway. He becomes very excited when the train emerges out of nowhere with full force. When aboard, he peers out of the window, transfixed. His expression is that of wonder. He quickly learns the names of all the stops and about the inter-connections. He studies the maps of New York and imagines going places in New York, and he studies the globe and the maps of the world. With his finger he traces lands to seas, imagining traveling in the world. When still older he sits by the window in his room and recites a prayer to drive away distractions that interfere with his studies: "Hashem (God) shall denounce you, O Satan, and Hashem, who selects Jerusalem, shall denounce you again."

My younger boy writes poems, and one of them is about the indifference of people towards a poor man selling pencils on the street. He also collects stones, and has a large collection of minerals from around the world. When he sees me work in the house he says, When I get older I will buy you beautiful things, beautiful jewelry. Once, when we were in Scotland, standing at the threshold of a forest, we saw the ground covered with moss, fresh and vital and dazzling, and he took my hand and put it over his chest and said, Feel how my heart beats. He loves rain and wind, and he takes walks in the rain without a raincoat or an umbrella. He won't wear a watch or take a key with him when he leaves the house. He likes to be as free as a nomad.

I continue with my studies in the seminar, constantly searching for time to read. When my boys nap I read. On my free day I read. As soon as I sit in the corner of the couch, my favorite seat, I read. I enjoy this time, borrowed time. I enjoy the solitude. The silence. I prepare my comments for class, and take extensive notes. Philosophers such as Samuel Alexander and Edmund Husserl are inscrutable on first reading but I don't give in. I venture upon unknown ideas, and I plough on. I picture Socrates, a gadfly, irritating people with his questions in his pursuit of truth. His sobering, subtle admonishment, "the unexamined life is not worth living," is making a dent in me.

I read large parts of two books every week. Never have ideas or lives of great people become alive to me in such a personal way. To think of time as temporal, everlasting, or eternal, gives me insight into the transient and enduring activities in my life. What are the occasions in my life that have been integrated and have had a lasting effect, and what are those that have been fleeting?

Endre Ady's poems strike me with their raw subjectivity,

> Hah, without hurt
> life would be

what holy, erotic storms
of fairest youth
are to a jaded courtesan,
a nothing[1]

Ady's poems, whose Jesus defiance, God intoxication, and sexual appetites awe me, describe the night as unfriendly, rejecting,

I would still not give you
a warm cover and pillow,
I would still not whisper
encouragement in your ear,
I would still remain
the nigh, nigh, Night.

The Night can only be the Night,
for the dying
are always dying
and this small life
is imperfect, dying, and weak[2]

How different from St. John of the Cross's Dark Night of the Soul, viewed by the author as "a happy chance" to purge the sense of the soul's lower part and bring it "into conformity with the spirit." Insight into these poems revives my interest in the Hebrew poetry of Bialik, Ibn Gabirol, and Yehuda Halevi, which seem to me—contrary to what I was taught—personal laments of the individual soul, rather than poems propelled by a religious or national spirit.

The idea of love in Plato's *Symposium*, the myriad points of view of Socrates' circle of philosophers, and the compelling voice of Socrates himself pique my interest. I am drawn to Aristophanes' graphic description of love. I imagine two halved bodies, two male halves or male and female halves, eventually meeting and uniting: "Man's original body having been thus cut in two, each half yearned for the half from which it had been severed."[3] To split is a punishment from heaven. To unite with our other half through the instruction of Love "gives us a sure

139

hope that, if we conduct ourselves well in the sight of heaven, he will hereafter make us blessed and happy by restoring us to our former state and healing our wounds."[4] The myth is functional, as all myths are. It brings to mind how the longing for what's lacking in us is often found in those we choose to associate with. Aristophanes' description is corporeal, fleshy. Love, Unity, and God are *not* without an image. I picture the Greek bodies in the same way I picture Adam's and Eve's, palpable and real as God walking in the Garden.

The lives of great religious personalities inspire me. The life of Jetsun Milarepa, the Tibetan Buddhist saint of the 11th century, and his *A Hundred Thousand Songs*, exhibit a spiritual journey entirely foreign to me, equally wondrous, and difficult enough for a Buddhist to last many, if not infinite, lifetimes. But Milarepa was able to realize the ultimate Buddhist goal of desirelessnes, Nirvana, in one lifetime. He abandons the use of black magic to avenge his relatives who harmed his family, and develops spiritual skills that afford him, paradoxically, to sever all attachments to things of the world, to people and to his own ego, while becoming compassionate towards others.

Of all the seminar books, *Life*, the autobiography of Saint Teresa of Avila, inspires me most. When I first read her I associate the depth of her Interior Castle, the stages of her spiritual life, with the depth of my sexuality. I was skeptical about the sincerity of her contrition concerning what seemed to me very small sins: her desire to be liked, and being vain in her youth. As I reread her, I am struck by her hospitable style, her subtle invitation to reflect on what she writes. I understand her spiritual greed, her need as an inspired nun to attend to her every thought and deed, her insatiable desire for contact with a higher realm of reality. I imagine her looking like the people in convents who, as Proust says, have a "brusque and cheerful" appearance, a "sublime face of true goodness,"[5] and who do not worry about hurting anybody. Teresa is not afraid to suffer, nor is she afraid to feel fervor, terror, and intense pleasure in the presence of God. Her prayer life awakens my spirit. Her way of perfection echoes in me unexpectedly, in an almost miraculous way, though I cannot implement what she does, or even get closer to implementing it.

Could I be as autonomous as Teresa? I am timid when my mother is angry with me. Or when others, who remind me of her, reprimand me. Lacking spontaneous anger—partly because I am an only child and have no experience in the squabbling, the retorts back and forth, all that siblings stuff—makes me think I am the perpetrator of my own confinement, the guard of the prison I devise for myself. I sometimes fear that I might offend people by disagreeing with them, or might say something that would hurt them. Once in a seminar I said something about Christianity that was disagreeable, and felt guilty towards a minister who was a member of the group. When Preston told me the minister would welcome such remarks, I was astonished. I learn that the seminars are dialectical, in the spirit of Plato's dialogues. By bringing personal thoughts and feelings into the discussion, the students engage in an exploration of ideas. The exposition of disparate beliefs and fallacies is expected.

In teaching the value of prayer Preston is at once serious and playful, never sanctimonious. He suggests that one can start a prayer life by praying for a taxi, and says he had a student who prayed to Hemingway. I learn from him to ask myself, in a moment of conflict, whether or not I would regret doing or not doing what I have in mind. In my sessions with Preston his appeal to truth is particularly strong. Most of the time I yield to his insights and his reasonable advice, which he generously gives. Preston urges me to stop being so polite, respond strongly to untruth. He says, It is better to do things or say things poorly, than not at all. (I learn that Preston is a Southerner from Baton Rouge, Louisiana, and that he once refused to break bread with a segregationist at a dinner table.)

Preston is insightful about my parents. He says, Your father was happy to be in the orphanage; what bothers your mother is that you don't think much of her. Preston thinks I am talented. He says that men like me for my character. He can tell I am proud from the way I walk and talk, and he refers to pride as a sin. Through him I discover that my marrying Mark had been spurred by seeing Preston in him, perhaps as soon as I saw Mark by the pool reading a thick book on Zen. Unwittingly, I sought Preston out.

After several years of study with Preston a friend of mine says that if I taught Interior Life Seminars she would attend. I cannot think of anyone with my background that would help me feel adequate to undertaking this awesome task. Who do I think I am, entering a territory that belongs to academia? What are my credentials? Your credentials are your soul, says Preston. He encourages me to teach the seminar. When I spread the word, twelve people sign up. I am assailed by doubts. I have visions of having the seminar in an empty room.

Having a career was never a viable option in my mind. When I attended the Academy of Music, I talked about being a piano teacher, but these were just words. When a piano teacher praised me for my playing, the praise dissipated, as if it were never said. I wanted to get married and have children, and the idea of working outside the home was a vague idea. If told I was attractive or straightforward, my mother believed it; I believed it. When my parents and I were at a party and they looked at me, I knew they were thinking I looked good. Later, my mother would tell me I looked the best. She liked to introduce me to her friends. She knew I would behave well and smile, and people would think I was pretty.

I am on her path. I follow in her footsteps. It doesn't occur to me I could have a path of my own. There were students in music school who seriously worked at what they were doing; they knew if you practiced hard enough you got results. But this eluded me. Of course, I did know that to succeed in an exam I had to study, that to play a piece of music I had to practice. But I didn't know that if I expended time and effort on my studies I could excel. And I didn't know that obstacles are part of the process, and that working through them, and feeling discouraged, and fearing to fail, is part of what one needs to endure in order to excel. I cannot picture myself as a professional. I do not think in terms of work as a vocational calling, or as something I would love to spend my time doing. Developing a career means meeting some impossible standards. I would be in turmoil; I'd be at sea, alone, unprotected; in the midst of the ocean, in a space without boundaries; I'd be away from shore, from my mother's wings; like a huge bird she stands with her wings open to shade me from the harm that would befall me if I stopped believing what she says—that I will not be a professor, or that too much studying is precarious. But in some strange way I don't believe her—there is the lure of risk, the craving to do new things, away from her outspread wings. Though life feels threatened, it propels me, and while I move forward I am haunted by the possibility of losing my past, all that is familiar and the people I love.

My ability to teach a seminar surprises me. In my first seminar everyone participates, they discuss the notions that have struck them most and apply them to their own lives. The love I feel for the books and the ideas is strong enough to surmount the difficulties I experience teaching: the long hours of preparation, struggling with incomprehensible ideas, recruiting people to join, feeling humiliated for not knowing the answer to a question, fearing that I might be "found out." In retrospect, at the end of the year, the students talk about the books they liked and didn't like, and how they have benefited from the discussions. I continue to teach the seminar year after year, often with the same people and with new ones as well.

During the year, summer notwithstanding, my contact with my parents consists of exchanging letters. My parents write often. I procrastinate. Sometimes I receive a letter from them admonishing me for not writing. On rare occasions I get a phone call from my father that lasts for only a couple of minutes in which he berates me for not writing. Sara, my Israeli friend in New York, inspires me to be confrontational with my parents. She confronts her mother with the spirit of a fighter. I follow her example and write my mother my grievances, one of which is that she stokes my guilt about having left Jerusalem. Writing the letter feels real. I put the letter in the mailbox and watch the lid close. For a moment I fear that neither my mother nor I, will survive the confrontation. But soon, the feeling of being true to myself overrides the fear.

I met Sara on a summer visit to Israel, at a friend's house in Tel Aviv. Sara is from a left-wing kibbutz. The left-wing youth movement in Jerusalem had its center in a cellar. It was a small group that discarded the "yoke" of religion. I envied their freedom. I imagined them progressive. A young woman from a left-wing kibbutz who rented a room from my next-door neighbor seemed to be an example of that freedom. Her language was crisp and direct, her clothes Bohemian yet simple. She said her mother was domineering, and I was impressed by her use of the word in English and by her attributing this characteristic to her mother; I unhesitatingly on the other hand kept things safe—I didn't dare think my mother was anything but a saint.

When I met Sara, I talked to her about people from the kibbutz. They are the best soldiers, I said. The kibbutz is like an army camp, she replied, and when you are in an army camp for twenty years it makes sense you will be a good soldier. Eventually I learnt that left-wing people are imprisoned by their socialist ideology. They are free from the mores of religion and the petite bourgeoisies, but they are tied to the kibbutz's ideology, and are not free to live life as individuals. Sara says, I will be coming to New York soon. I ask her to call me.

As soon as I meet Sara in New York I feel close to her. Our intimacy, our confiding in each other, reminds me of my friendships in Jerusalem. Sara makes New York her home. On a couple of occasions we take vacations together. I remember the morning light one winter, pouring into the house my husband and I and Sara rent for a week in Puerto Rico. Early in the morning Sara takes our sons for a swim in the ocean. They come back looking happy and revitalized. In the afternoon we make an excursion to San Juan. Trailing Mark through the winding streets one day—he walks very fast—I feign a leg injury to slow him down. He is concerned, and for the rest of the day we continue at a slower pace. Later, sitting in the spacious courtyard of a hotel with regal palm trees and ornate balconies, having exotic drinks, I tell him it is all a joke. Sara and I laugh about it long after.

With Sara as a friend, New York is more companionable and habitable. Sara and I speak in Hebrew. She tells me about her difficult experiences as a child, growing up in the children's house in the kibbutz, separated from her mother. She tells me about the self-righteousness of kibbutz members, whose ideology overrides human feelings, and where any dissent in opinion is considered traitorous. I tell her about my upbringing, which forced religion on me, and my guilt about any religious transgression. Sara also participates in my seminar, and like me she appreciates expanding her knowledge. That she and I share a language, a concern about events in Israel, and discuss new ideas that issue from seminar study, mitigates my loneliness.

13

"I HAVE NO WORLD BUT ONE"

Mark and I rent a downtown loft to use as a work space. Mark has turned to portrait photography, so he uses the space for shooting and printing. I use my space to teach the seminar and to write. It's here, in my refuge, where I write poems, where I feel the freedom I always longed for, not bound to anyone's requirements or tastes. Feeling free to say what I see, say it exactly how I see it or feel it. I write, I rewrite, I give form to my experience, as if I am learning to play flamenco guitar: a phrase comes to mind, I write it, I pause, I revise. I pray for a flow of words to *become* the experience. Sometimes I pace in my room and pray for one word, a single word that will express precisely what I want to say. I feel like Hayim Nahman Bialik who says,

> I have no world but one
> the world that is in my heart.[1]

The shelves are filled with books (Books are good people, Preston said once), and it is a thrill to walk by them, pick up a book, leaf through it, read a line or two.

Spending time alone writing helps me pay attention to subtle inner changes. When I discover a feeling I didn't know I had, or when I do something I've never done before, or when I have helped someone in need, I say, thank you God for giving me that capacity. I consider myself successful when I better understand a poem by Rilke.

When I was eleven, my girlfriends and I wrote and composed songs at my piano. Living in a world of our own making was paradisiacal. As a teenager I was banished from that world, perhaps because my mother ignored those early bursts of creativity and I had no permission and example to continue on this path; or perhaps because my social life, my friendships, and my crushes were too much with me.

In my poetry workshop at the 92nd Street Y, after struggling for eight weeks to write something that could stand as a poem, the teacher says, Your poem is perfect. But things didn't start out that way. At first, the teacher was very critical of my work. I cried when I left class, and later I showed the poem to Preston. In the chaos of my words he was able to see a spark, and he said, I studied at LSU when Robert Penn Warren and Cleanth Brooks were there; screw the Y, I know poetry, and you are on your way.

One afternoon I go to bed and cover my body and my head with a blanket. My first poem has been published. Under the blanket I am protected from experiencing an assault on my routine life. I feel a mingling of excitement and fear over something unknown that is about to happen. I'm reminded of the time in kindergarten when I couldn't find the apron I was embroidering, and for a few days, when the sewing class took place, I hid in the bathroom.

After a few years of writing I discover the poems of Louis Simpson. His poem *My Father in the Night Commanding No* particularly moves me,

> My father in the night commanding No
> Has work to do. Smoke issues from his lips;
>   He reads in silence.
> The frogs are croaking and the streetlamps glow.
>
> And then my mother winds the gramophone;
> The Bride of Lammermoor begins to shriek—
>   Or reads a story—
> About a prince, a castle, and a dragon[2]

How does Simpson create such lyricism with simple words? I want Simpson to comment on my poetry. Sara encourages me to approach him. I do. He graciously agrees. In my awkward first poems he sees potential. He points out my weaknesses and my strengths, which show me the direction I will follow. He has been an inspiration ever since.

While doing the assignments for the seminar, it is heartwarming to come across places in the New Testament that are familiar to me. The tiny, inconspicuous opening to the Church of the Nativity in Bethlehem is not only the entrance to the church my father and I visited when I was a child, but was also the entrance to the barn where Jesus was born and adored by the Magi. I write of an early experience in that church,

> Years later, when I was a little girl,
> my father took me to a church to listen to a choir
> and gaze at the quiet candles lit in a vaulted hall.
> We watched the permanent fact of loss in a painted figure[3]

And Kefar Nahum, a place by the sea of Galilee that Mark and I visited on our honeymoon—a place I looked at with unopened eyes—rises from its tiny plot of land with an Italianate church, and becomes the home for many of Jesus' miracles. My poem describing an encounter with a priest there is preceded by my being with Mark,

> "Lovely and Loved"
> you rest your head on my lap,
> you and I in this room
> this sort of wonder
> is beautifully unexplained . . .
>
> Within us hums of a conch-shell
> humming sounds of inane lives which
> were never fulfilled. But the priest
> cups our hands in his palms:
> the least seed will sprout, yellow
> and tall, full grain in a sunny field.[4]

Another place I come across in the reading is the Mount of Olives, where my mother's father and my father's ancestors were buried. (In 1967, when Israel recaptured the Old City, my parents searched for the burial places of their family, but their tombs, among others, were not found.)

The Mount takes on a special mystery when I discover the Garden of Gethsemane, where Jesus prayed before his crucifixion, is at its foot. I am curious about these non-Jewish holy places, but they evoke no reverence in me. Jerusalem, with its rich historical past, remains the city whose beauty is in its dust and its alleys, and whose memory is in my blood,

> The Mount of Olives split in half,
> and since my first departure
> I lie in the huge gorge that was formed,
> I lie on one side, then on the other,
> to find my self[5]

I am busy raising my boys and there are chores to do. Guilt-evoking letters from my parents keep coming. It is difficult to get all the reading done for two seminars, one given by Preston, and one by me. Responsibilities are accompanied by anxiety. Decisions are difficult. I am often at a loss about what I should do. Preston says, Who is attacking you? Who are the people who don't want you to know what to do? Hearing this, I am sometimes even more at a loss. But I find myself in writing.

I enjoy seeing my boys grow. And I enjoy the freedom to assimilate ideas in philosophical and especially in religious writings that are foreign to me, religions that were never imposed upon me. Because I am not forced to practice them, I am able to see them clearly, I understand their value, and begin to understand the value of religion in general. With Preston as a teacher, new ideas are acts of kindness; they refuse to be narrow. I no longer have a sense of aimlessness, nor do I feel defeated by loneliness as I did during my formal student days.

Reading Wittgenstein, who does not take shortcuts to the truth, is a challenge. His breathless writing is often lost on me; I comprehend its beauty, but I need to read and reread it to comprehend its essence. I think of what he says, "It is not *how* things are in the world that is mystical, but *that* it exists."[6] It gladdens me that Wittgenstein points out something we take for granted, the mystery of the "is" of the world. I, too, think that the mystery of creation, the mystery of God, as mysterious as it is, is less of a mystery.

There are moments in which I feel kinship with Buddhism, realizing what it is like to be detached from desire, to be attuned to the idea of "no name and fame." I picture Buddha under the Nigrodha tree, for seven weeks he is without bodily wants, nourished by the joys of contemplation. He is desireless: free from distractions and liberated from suffering. If I could only have such a sudden awakening, perfecting an answer to agony. There are moments when I accept the idea of having to bear my cross, whatever it may be.

My seminar and my writing are my work, which I love, and am committed to. I don't think of my work in terms of a career. Inside me I feel increasingly alive. I am interested in the interior spirit that is active and charts its own way, and am in awe of the spirit of the living creatures in Ezekiel's mysterious vision, transmitted to the wheels of gleaming chrysolite beside them, so that when the living creatures rise from the ground, the wheels rise, too.

At parties, with parents of my children's friends, and in the building where I live, though I adapt, I have a sense of standing apart. I do not share nursery songs, TV shows, or politics with Americans. I don't approach the American Civil War, which we study in Preston's seminar, with the same curiosity other students do, nor am I concerned about the upheavals of the '60s, not even as a bystander. I am still captivated by news from Israel.

One day I walk by a courtyard and I see a group of people dressed in black. It is morning, and it is the morning of the eve of Passover. Jews are burning hametz. And a memory without words or images, a memory plain and naked without a sound, taste, or smell, wells up in me. Is this memory of my heritage the answer I am looking for? I search for an image of my father burning the hametz, but I cannot find him or a trace of him. I cannot find the sound of his voice, I cannot hear or smell the fire burning. The people in the courtyard are blessing God, who has sanctified us by His commandments, and commanded us concerning the removal of hametz. He has commanded these people dressed in black, and He has commanded me. And though these people are strangers to me, I do know them, since we share this commandment, since we share this commandment from a time we cannot remember, but that we remember nevertheless.

Slowly an image of my father emerges. Before Passover he and I climbing up to the semi-dark attic below our red-tiled roof, where we store our Passover dishes in a black chest. From the attic window I look out and see a sea of red-tiled roofs that stretches as far as the market. My father and I kneel by the chest and my father opens it slowly. I am wonder-struck by the delicious secrets that are unveiled: ceramic ware, cork and china, vases and pots, all more beautiful than any other dishes or utensils used during the year. An otherworldly mood settles in. Little by little, very carefully, and with the help of a flashlight, we unpack the dishes. I feel liberated. This is my journey from exile back home, from the dull rooms downstairs to the alluring attic, where beauty and adventure reign.

I also remember my father giving me a small Purim *megillah* (a scroll, especially of the book of Esther, read aloud on Purim) covered with bluish-purple velvet cloth embroidered in gold thread, and the little ebony hand that goes with it. I can still feel the thrill of looking at the megillah and touching it, knowing it is mine. And I recall my father fasting on Tisha B'Av, to remember the destruction of the temples in Jerusalem, and going with him to the Wailing Wall, a remnant of the Temple, and praying by the wall, and kissing the stone, believing it has a special power that will help us get what we want.

The news of the 1973 war in Israel comes upon us suddenly, and gives my family a terrible jolt. A couple of months earlier we visited Jerusalem, and there were no signs of war. Then on the day of Yom Kippur the Egyptians attack Israel from across the Suez Canal, and the Syrians from the north. I am frozen in terror and in guilt. Living in New York while Israel is at war makes me feel small, blurred, a nothing. Can Israel survive the attack? We keep hearing about the fear, terror, and panic there, and about the fallen soldiers. I participate in a protest—something I usually loathe doing—which takes place in Riverside Park. Then Israel counter-attacks. There is a turn of events. The war ends. The country has survived yet another war.

I feel euphoric, as all of Israel does, when Sadat arrives a few years later in Jerusalem, seeking to make peace. But the excitement soon fades. I am demoralized as Israel settles into the hard realization that in spite of glimpses of hope, the conflict with the Arabs is not going away any day soon.

A month before the 1973 war Dina says, Why don't you give a seminar in Jerusalem? There is a feeling of uncertainty in the country, a spiritual void. In me, the feeling is conflicted. On the one hand, I feel a duty to teach and transmit what I've learned, on the other, I dread it. My sense of obligation wins over, and the year after the war, I give a seminar. Eleven women sign up, mostly Dina's friends, and some of mine.

Before my visit I prepare a reading list and send seminar books to Jerusalem. On my visit with my two boys, my parents meet us at the airport with a basket of fruit, water, and juice. Dina comes along with her two boys. We are excited to see each other, exchanging quick reports.

I take my boys, who are now nine and seven years old, to shop for sandals, Israeli-made sandals that are the best looking and the most comfortable. We go to the center of town, Jaffa Road, where most of the shops are. Looking at shop windows in the Columns' Building, the imposing shopping center with its grand columns, I remember the town whore who stood or sat on the corner of the street, always in the same spot, knitting. Her hair was unkempt. Her clothes sagged. When she smiled she showed a few broken teeth. They said she took her clients to Mamila Park.

I also take my children to different playgrounds, as well as to different swimming pools. The swimming pool at the King David Hotel is surrounded by a flower garden with a view of the Edom Mountains. I remember how once I danced tango with my fiancé in the bar of the hotel. Though it was just before my engagement was broken, my love for him had not yet waned, and our dance stirred up sensuous expectations through every pore of my body.

As I take walks in the city and its outskirts I carry a notebook and scribble notes, which I later develop into poems,

> An eagle spreads its wings
> above the valley where each house
> is a white validation.
>
> But I prefer to go elsewhere,
> like to Natan Birenbaum Street
> where a nettle-like bush leans
> on a crooked wall and children use cartons for toys.[7]

I am well prepared for teaching the seminar. I leave nothing to chance. But before the first seminar begins, an emotional paralysis takes over me. I lie on the couch feeling numb, a floating anxiety. Everything outside is nonexistent. Dina comes over and reassures me that everyone is eager to attend the seminar. I think of Wittgenstein, who left everything to chance and thought aloud in front of his students.

I fear that somebody will label me a heretic for studying and teaching religions not my own. I look for authoritative backing in Jewish resources for my "straying." I discover that rabbis in antiquity thought highly of Avnimos the Gardi, the Greek heathen philosopher, and that Avnimos befriended Rabbi Meir, the great Tanna (a sage, one of the writers of the Mishna). Rabbi Meir continued to study with his teacher Elisha ben Avuyah, even after the latter abandoned Judaism and became an apostate. I remember the terror I felt as a schoolgirl at the mentioning of Elisha ben Avuyah. We thought of him as a rebel, an anathema, spiteful and strange. His name became synonymous with pronouncing God's holy name in vain. He was called Aher ("the other"). We never talked about him as one of the great sages, nor did we discuss why he renounced Judaism. We didn't even scorn the corrupt kings of Israel, who openly worshipped other gods in the same contemptuous way. In a class about the history of the Jews, we rushed through the passages about Jesus, whom we called by his Hebrew name, Yeshua. I considered Jesus and John the Baptist, whose Hebrew name was Yochanan Hamatbil, strangely deviant. They interrupted the flow of history. They were peripheral, yet figures to be wary of.

The weekly seminar, which lasts six weeks, seems to leave an indelible impression on people. All in all, it goes better than I expected. Everyone shows up every week, and everyone participates. One person tells me that she is so stimulated by the ideas she cannot sleep. For most it's a new experience: developing an interest in religions other than Judaism. The form of the seminar, calling on everyone to talk, and agreeing to disagree during the discussion, is new as well. Bonhoeffer's *Letters and Papers from Prison* echoes with everyone. No one ever heard of this German minister who in 1939 returned to Germany from New York to resist Hitler. And all are struck by his fearlessness. There are other readings of unknown materials, such as Confucius and Milarepa and Peirce; even Plato's *Symposium* is a first read for some. There are two people who are hostile to the material, consistently finding fault with it. I feel detached about their reactions. But I am anxious about responding to questions and accurately transmitting what I know.

I spend sleepless nights praying to have the courage to continue the seminar. As I lie in bed, I appeal to Teresa of Avila and Milarepa—my invisible community—who endured worldly attacks. On the one hand the appeals infuse me with courage. But on the other, appealing to Milarepa, the Buddhist saint, and petitioning the Christian saint Teresa, in the city where I was taught that praying to saints is idol worship, increases my guilt.

I imagine Milarepa thin, wiry, determined, and alive, more like a spirit than a man. He is the quintessential exotic pilgrim. I think of his frustration with his guru in the early days of his discipleship, the affection he had for his guru's wife and her affection for him. I can see him meditating on severing all attachments, letting go of his ego. He roams around naked in his cave, his body green from eating nothing but nettles. I imagine his bones quivering with struggle and joy. His songs soar with disdain for the world and its objects. And I envision Teresa of Avila praying ceaselessly, passionately, renouncing pleasures of the world.

Nothing stops her—not the attacks of Christian authorities, nor her inner struggles—from building eighteen convents that subscribe to her reform: Convents are no longer a place for conversations and for socialization, but for prayer and contemplation. For Teresa, God is enough. She rejoices in Him. But I experience joy as fleeting. It is almost nonexistent.

Strangely enough, I like to come home after the seminar and talk to my parents (it is my father who is most interested to hear about it). I am glad they are awake. I sit on the edge of their bed and tell them about the class. My parents have mixed feelings. They raise objections when they see my books on Christianity and Buddhism, but for the most part they restrain themselves from criticizing me. My father at first thinks I have a "bug" in my head, but then says, Why are you anxious? You are giving people something good. My parents are busy caring for their new apartment, which they moved to a couple of years before. It is spacious, airy, and full of light, with a view of the Judean Hills. They install a telephone so my friends can reach me. They also install another bathroom on one of the terraces, and they buy an additional refrigerator, to make my visits with my children more comfortable.

Back in New York, I feel less anxious than when I was in Jerusalem. I feel safe. Walking on Broadway one day, I feel my head splitting at the top of my skull. It is a vivid experience, a brutal reaction to the fact that I have given a seminar in Jerusalem and survived. The cost was high. It's one I can now bear.

14

THE SUN SETTING ON THE HUDSON RIVER

Preston's students know he suffers from asthma. He often tells us about his attacks and the reason for them. He says, My unconscious picks up when people's conduct is not consonant with how they feel. For instance, he continues, I was in a meeting with a group of psychoanalysts, and I got asthma because the people there were all smiles and courteous to each other, but underneath there was envy and ill will. He also tells us that he doesn't pray for himself, except for his asthma. One day, we are informed that there will be no psychoanalytical sessions and no seminar that week because Preston had a serious asthma attack and is hospitalized. He returns to work a few weeks later. That summer he calls our house and says, I would like to bring you the tapes of the retreats. He comes over with a suitcase and gives us the tapes. It is clear that he wants us to have these tapes as a resource for future work. We have been studying with Preston for ten years, and feel committed to continue his work and add to his legacy. We say to him that we would like to publish a journal based on his teachings. He says, It is a good idea.

A year later, in one of the seminars Preston says, Something is wrong with my mind, I need to see a doctor. He continues to complain about not remembering the assignments he assigns for seminar. He forgets appointments. After being hospitalized again for an undisclosed reason Preston is diagnosed with Alzheimer's disease. It's 1975, and few have heard of this disease. I am in shock. Everyone in seminar is in shock. Seminar members anxiously ask doctors and whoever might know for information about the disease. Doctors tell us that Alzheimer's some-times hits people who are not old. We think it is an irony that a brain disease hits a person as brilliant as Preston, who is only fifty years old. Preston's family sends him to Baton Rouge to be cared for by his mother. I feel a great sorrow. I miss him, the riches of his knowledge. I miss his guidance and support, his teaching. To my surprise, I also feel relief. I am released from his commanding presence and words, the constant push to stretch my capacity. There are others in the group who are angry at Preston and want to separate from his legacy. Do they feel abandoned? I cannot say for certain—I am only in touch with those who continue to be interested in his work.

Mark and I visit Preston McLean in his hometown six months later. He is in a helpless state, nonetheless he is happy to see us. His mother makes a dinner with a delicious pecan pie for dessert. We take a walk, and watch people playing tennis. Preston points to the players and says, They too have a world hypothesis, and adds, Tennis is about killing the other person. When we come back to the house Preston's mother does most of the talking. She says, My husband left us when Preston was three years old, and I suspect he died of Alzheimer's. There is no self-pity or tinge of complaint in her voice. All business, she attends to Preston, her only child, with loving care. Preston says very little. He surprises us when he says, "Books are good people," a line we repeat on our way home. On our next visit, a year later, Preston doesn't recognize us. In a poem, I refer to him as having been a blazing Stoic light, and add,

> And a cloud veils your words,
> and your words disconnected from the world,
> and your thoughts disconnected from your words,
> and your words disconnected from the world
> which accuses you.[1]

I continue to teach a weekly seminar. The size of my group varies, from three to twelve people. The work is serious, and there is a sense of commitment. There is no drama. Every person is given a chance to talk, which helps to sharpen thinking and speaking skills, and encourages those reluctant to talk. Each year I concentrate on a different topic. I might focus one year on deistic religions, Christianity, Judaism, and Zoroastrianism, and in another, on non-deistic religions, Buddhism, and Confucianism. I add books in philosophy, psychology, and poetry.

When Preston was well I introduced him and my class to *The Path of the Just* by Moshe Chayim Luzzatto—an eighteenth century Jewish rabbi and Kabbalist—a book Preston found so illuminating he sent copies to six of his Jewish friends in Baton Rouge. The ideas in Luzzatto's book become meaningful, like other ideas discussed in seminar, by application to life. One idea in particular stands out: "Humility in thought consists in a person's reflecting upon and recognizing as a truth the fact that he does not deserve praise and honor (let alone elevation above his fellow men), both because of his natural limitations and because of his accumulated defects."[2]

I continue to introduce other books, mostly from Preston's reading list. A.N.Whitehead's philosophy is difficult to penetrate, but worth the effort. The idea of individuality in community, which Whitehead writes about in *Religion in the Making*, stirs up a discussion: "The world is a scene of solitariness in community. The individuality of entities is just as important as their community. The topic of religion is individuality in community."[3] I mull over the implications of maintaining individuality in community and the complications it entails, the need to be ruthless and stake out the territory of a solitary world to prevent others from trespassing.

At that time, Mark, an avid WBAI listener, tells me that the radio station is looking for someone to do poetry programs. The opportunity to do something different, to get out in the world and meet poets I admire, excites me. I make an appointment with Rick Harris, the head of the Art Department. With Rick's guidance I begin working at this left-wing radio station. I produce poetry programs—interviewing poets and writers, and recording them reading their poems. The station, on 8th Avenue and 34th Street, has a neglected appearance—a long, dark corridor as you enter, small rooms that are poorly lit, littered with papers, and spotty rugs. To some in the station, anarchy is seen as a necessary good. Producers have the freedom to produce what they want, and the voices on the air are unpolished and untrained, as are the words they utter. But the programs are shot through with glimpses of truth, a keen awareness of revolutionary groups in downtrodden societies such as in Nicaragua and in South Africa. I think that despite my capacity to adapt and to get along with people, I am, like the others here, an outcast, a marginal person, with an affinity for the countercultural parts of society. Why else would

I be so comfortable in an atmosphere adverse to worldliness? And my attraction to religion and the life of the spirit, does it not embody a desire to shun the world?

I interview mostly poets and a few writers. Several are Israeli. When the poet Seamus Heaney arrives at the radio station he carries a suitcase tied with a belt. My daughter gave this to me, he says, pointing mischievously to the belt. Heaney exudes warmth. His hair is tussled, and a twinkle in his eye speaks of a good-natured, unpretentious soul. Before being interviewed Heaney asks to see the questions. He passes a quick judgment and agrees. Heaney explains his interior quest for "the growth of a poet's mind" as a religious pilgrimage, and as part of that pilgrimage, he writes about a "Freckle-face, fox-head, pod of the broom..." a girl whom he chose at a game of "secrets" when "playing houses" as a child. He reads from his poem in his Irish, lilting, musical way,

> As if I knelt for years at a keyhole
> Mad for it, and all that ever opened
> Was the breathed-on grille of a confessional
> Until that night I saw her honey-skinned
> Shoulder-blades and the wheatlands of her back
> Through the wide keyhole of her keyhole dress
> And a window facing the deep south of luck
> Opened and I inhaled the land of kindness[4]

I am partial to the poetry of Czeslaw Milosz, which also has religious overtones, and I want to interview him. Mark has a photography show in Riverside, California, and a few days later he drives me to Milosz's home in Berkeley. At the door I ask Milosz whether Mark should wait to take me back to the train. Milosz gazes at me and says, Let's dismiss him, I'll drive you the train. Milosz is a handsome seventy-year-old, with gracious European manners. His study is filled with books and bears an aura of serious thought. The interview, which refers only to the content of his poetry, captures Milosz's interest, and he responds to my questions with an unusual open mind. As he reads I feel a kinship with him,

> And disobedient, curious, on the first step to Hell,
> Easily enticed by the newest idea[5]

And,

> Sometimes believing, sometimes not believing,
> With others like myself I unite in worship[6]

When Milosz drives me to the train and discovers I am from Israel, he says, I learnt Hebrew and translated the Psalms from Hebrew into Polish; my Israeli friends say my Hebrew is good. Learning a new language at this late age and translating biblical Hebrew into another language is quite a feat. I regret I didn't suggest to speak Hebrew with him; I think he would have liked to. In the car, contrary to how I felt while I interviewed him, I was self-conscious and tense.

During this time of seminar teaching a faint longing for my religion surfaces, and I find myself drawn to visiting various synagogues. Once, on Yom Kippur, on our way home from a walk in the park, my older son, who is home from college, and I, pass by the Carlebach Shul, a small Hasidic synagogue. I say, Let's go in and see what's it's like. We enter the synagogue and stand in the back. The small space is shabby in appearance, the paint is peeling, the floor broken in places, the ark and the pulpit are old. The rabbi, Shlomo Carlebach, is vibrant. He stands solidly, his gaze is direct, and what he says sounds improvisational, not rehearsed or spoken to make an impression. My son is especially inspired by his words, "Religion is life."

The rabbi sings. The congregation sings with him. The singing is enthusiastic, a chorus rising in joyful unison that seems to open the gates of heaven, break a barrier to God's mercy. The tone of the service, the entire atmosphere, is very different from the Yom Kippur service of my youth, which was solemn and sorrowful. There is rhythmic clapping, feverish dancing. Men and women in separate circles dance and stomp the floor in praise and in worship, each step as if communing something mysterious, inexpressible in any other way.

I begin to attend the synagogue on the Sabbath and on Jewish holidays. In this humble, unpretentious, informal environment, the walls are imbued with years of prayerful songs. As I pray, I sense within me generations of people who prayed these prayers for centuries. To this synagogue one comes to plead and give thanks. There is freedom given to parishioners to practice religion on their own level, no pressure to be anybody but who you are, no dress code, no special honor or respect given to those who are rich. Sometimes a woman walks in wearing slacks or a dress open at the neck—in most Orthodox synagogues this would be frowned upon, her appearance would be considered "immodest." Not here. A man wearing overalls with tens of different political buttons pinned to his hat and clothing is not rejected. No one is. There is recognition that protestations before God accompanied by love, are what is needed to get closer to Him. This speaks to me. Perhaps because I am a descendant of Hasidim—both my grandfathers were Hasidim—the life of the spirit has been, unwittingly, passed on to me.

I buy a lulav and ethrog, and attend the synagogue on Sukkot. Under the leafy roof of the Sukkah I direct the lulav to the six different directions, as required, and I bless it. I bless the ethrog and endow it with warmth. It becomes an object of love, like the ethrog encased in a wooden box my father gave me as a child. My husband, who comes along with me on this day, and I, sit in the Sukkah having a Kiddush. Mark has visited the synagogue before, mostly on Rosh Hashanah and Yom Kippur, but does not care to attend regularly. He says, I don't read Hebrew and cannot follow the prayers. Rabbi Eli Chaim, Shlomo's twin, who officiates in the synagogue when Shlomo is away giving concerts, is very fond of Mark, and he once asks him why he doesn't attend services more often. Mark says, half in jest, When you come to *my* "shul" to see an exhibition of my work, I'll come to yours.

It rains in the Sukkah. Shlomo asks the people around the table to stay. He talks about the close relationship the shtetl water carrier, a simple man, had with God, and extols the ignorant man, who couldn't read the prayers but communed by whistling. I enjoy the feeling that God is in the ethrog and the lulav, and in the branches on top of the Sukkah, needing no proofs, nor a rational foundation. I like the idea of getting closer to God through a simple heart, through raising the eyes upward, through sitting in a Sukkah while it rains, and letting myself get wet.

The study of other religions has evoked in me astonishment, wonder, and love for great personalities of all religions crystallized into a simple thirst for God. In the synagogue, I weep and submit my prayers to the wrathful, loving Jewish God whom I used to pray to as a child, the God who, I believed, was outside my window in His imageless body, above the lone cypress tree and the steadfast sky. Clothed with new meanings, personal meanings, the Hebrew letters, the verses and phrases of the prayer book, are revived.

It would take me many years to be free to confess my sins, to discover the more subtle sins, to realize that anxiety is harmful, a kind of a sin; to feel that I deserve God's forgiveness for what I think of as my sins, and to genuinely ask His forgiveness for the sins I've committed against my children—being anxious, overbearing, overprotective.

On one Sabbath, Sara visits the synagogue. The visit is a good experience for her. We continue to attend every Sabbath and Jewish holiday. We are touched by Shlomo's authenticity, moved by his seeing holiness in poverty, secularism, disheveled people, joy. Once at a Kiddush, when Shlomo talked about the Bible portion of the week, a young man, obviously retarded, mumbled incoherently. Shlomo responded to him tenderly, You are holy, very holy. Shlomo speaks his mind fearlessly, not accountable to any person. He is critical of religious fanaticism and mainstream clichés, and of any religious practice that is insincere. For me, Preston has redeemed religion, and Shlomo is redeeming Judaism. He views God as tender, and quotes the Baal Shem Tov, advising the father whose son has abandoned God, "Love him more than ever!"

For Shlomo the Sabbath is more than the seventh day, the day of rest. It is the quintessence of Judaism, the sweetness in life. Friday nights he greets the Sabbath as a Bride, a Queen. "Come O Bride, Come O Bride" he sings as a lover, gently, never in a hurry, greeting the Sabbath with a kiss, courting the Sabbath as if it were indeed a queen, a bride. In these moments the Sabbath is no longer the law that inspires fear in me, a day I resent and want to flee from, but a day founded on the life of God, who seceded from work on the seventh day, and who "will come and rest on the whole stretch of Mount Zion." The Sabbath in these moments is a gift—I delight in it, I open it gently, with care, with mindfulness, lovingly looking in to see what is inside, and I contemplate its contents: the promise not only of rest, but of renewal. The Sabbath is a gift that could be received the way the Kabbalists did by going to a field and closing their eyes to identify with the Shechinah, the Divine Presence, who lost her sight by weeping for the exile of Israel.

At home, inspired by Shlomo, I discover that certain Jewish religious rituals give me respite. I pause to light the Sabbath candles on Friday night. I cover my head with a scarf and I cover my face with my hands. A calm settles in the room, and I can hear the silence inside me. I begin the ritual not by praying for myself or for my family, but by reciting with a still voice the blessing I am commanded to recite, blessing God for commanding me to light the candles. I recall the Divine Presence in Jerusalem resting on the roofs of houses before the Sabbath when, for a moment, all was space and breath. From my window I see the sun setting on the Hudson River, the sky reddening, a boat gliding by in an eternal moment.

Before the meal I bless God for commanding me to bless the wine, and I ritually wash my hands, remaining silent. Then I slice the Challah and bless the bread. I have chosen to welcome the Sabbath not by observing all the rules, but by following those that engage my spirit. My husband is a silent participant. He looks forward to these Friday nights at home, not accepting any invitations to go out, and enjoying a more elaborate meal than usual. The next day, solitary, on my way to the synagogue, I am already in a mood of prayer. There is power in saying "Shema" with the community, looking outward before the word becomes flesh, before it solidifies within.

Mark, Kathie (also a student of Preston whom we met in seminar), and I work in accordance with Preston's wishes on transcribing his teachings from tapes he had given us, recorded in seminars and retreats. The work is technically tedious. But we delight in the ideas. We marvel at how precise, enlightening, and relevant they are. We enjoy listening to Preston's voice. We share memories of retreats and seminars.

In 1984 we receive the sad news that Preston died. Mark and I arrange a small memorial in our house in which people read from Preston's favorite books. The atmosphere is one more of reverence than of mourning. By then, our grieving has already been done.

PART III

APPLES DIPPED IN HONEY

My two sons, after graduating college, almost simultaneously become ultra-religious. Did they absorb my love for religion while still in the womb, or in my arms when they were infants? They are proud of their ancestor Reb Shmelke from Nikolsburg, who is depicted in Buber's stories as a man who dismissed pretense and current opinions, and was devoted to the pursuit of truth in its most naked and humble form. On the Day of Atonement, "he sang new melodies, miracle of miracles, which he had never heard and which no human ear had ever heard; and he did not even know what he was singing, and what melody he was singing, for he clung to the upper world."[1] I think of Mordecai Schnitzer, another ancestor on my father's side, the first artist in Palestine, who like Reb Shmelke, clung to the upper realms of existence. How else can one explain the permission to cross conventional boundaries of orthodoxy—the energy to create art, the shift from community to artistic individualism, and back to community working as a caretaker—but that these gifts were inspired by the Divine?

My sons visit the grave of Reb Shmelke in the Ukraine to pay him homage. Though they are not Hasidim—they belong to the Mitnagdim sect that is considered more intellectual—they adopt their religious practice with the same enthusiasm that is reflected in Hasidic practice. They describe their religious experiences in the same way my husband and I describe our psychoanalytical and seminar experiences when we say that there was a life before these experiences, and a life after. They cannot imagine how they lived without the clarity, the commitment, and the dedication these disciplines require in order to evolve.

I remember my sons as children, playing together with large wooden blocks for hours at a time. Once when we visited Scotland we left them at a beach in front of our inn to go shopping. When we returned hours later we saw they had built a sand city, about 15 square meters big. Though very different in temperament (from birth my older son was happy where he was, while my younger son was restless), and though they have always led separate social lives and ultimately settled in different countries (one in Israel and the other in England), their choices and their ways of life have similarities. In their late twenties they would both marry religious women and have similarly sized families. They don't stay in close touch, but they respect, love, and speak well of each other.

As I prepare apples and honey for the festive meal on Rosh Hashanah, I think of my younger son. As a teenager he showed an inkling of what would develop into his great love of the Jewish tradition—he arranged various symbolic foods and recited short liturgical prayers alluding to them: carrots for the increase of merits, leeks for the destruction of our enemies, beets for the removal of our adversaries, dates for the consummation of our enemies, a gourd to tear the decree of our sentence and for the proclamation of our merits before God, the pomegranate to increase our merits as the seeds of a pomegranate, fish to be fruitful as fish, the head of a fish so that we can be as the head and not as the tail, and an apple dipped in honey so that our year be sweet.

I think of my younger son's love for apples and I can almost sense his scent, the scent of an apple orchard. I remember how he would scoop seeds from a pomegranate and serve it to us in a small bowl. Once, my son, who has a flair for ceremony, prepared, together with his older brother, an elaborate meal for us for our wedding anniversary, and created a "harem" in the living room, with couches and pillows and screens. I think of him arranging that celebration and remember his twelfth birthday on an island in Scotland. All day, as my husband and I and our two boys were busy touring the beach, "the singing sands" as it is called, doing chores in our rented stone croft, washing our clothes in a stream, our younger son waited for us to remember his birthday. That evening he told us he had woken up in the morning thinking that his room would be filled with balloons. I can still see his blue eyes sad against the sky at sunset filled with red and pink, and I can still feel a shudder inside me.

I've been attending The Carlebach Shul for some time. I am disciplined—

I pray the morning prayers, and read the Psalms and the Tanya. I resort to prayer at all times of the day wherever I am—on the street, on the subway, in my bed before I go to sleep. Prayer puts me in touch with what I want, it breaks a vicious cycle, it cleanses my soul. I tell God what pains me and what delights me, my envy, my ill will, my visions of a catastrophe, my love, my compassion, my joy.

My sons' religious practice enhances my Jewish spiritual sensibility. I have a community with them. When we visit with each other and spend a Sabbath together, they discuss passages from the weekly portion of the Torah. I keep a glatt-kosher home for their sake, as I want them to eat at my house when they visit. It is also a way of reconciling with my religious background, which in spite of having been forced on me, helps to provide the soil for, and my delight in, the religious spirit.

One night, in the winter of 1989, I have a dream about my childhood neighbors in Jerusalem sitting in their home on couches, dressed in their best clothes. There is an ephemeral beauty to their house; transparent curtains hang from the ceiling. They welcome me and invite me to sit with them. I say, I will join you soon. I go back to my childhood house where my parents are lying on the floor sleeping. I am worried and afraid to wake up my father. My mother's eyes are closed; she opens them when I lift her up.

A few weeks later, while in the synagogue, I feel chilled. I pray with my coat on in the corner of the synagogue. At home I take a nap, and in my dream someone is plucking the flesh off my face, tearing it to pieces. The phone rings and the voice of my parents' neighbor in Jerusalem says, Your father is in critical condition, take a plane to Israel tonight.

On the flight to Israel, my younger son beside me, I consider that my father may be dead. When I arrive at my parents' building, glaring at me on a column at the entrance is the announcement of his death: "May his memory live forever." I have seen many announcements like this when I was growing up, glued on billboards; the name of the dead person speaks of anguish, and the names of the family members speak of heartbreak. When I see my father's name I am in shock—he is already transmigrating, moving away from this city he was so much a part of, the city, which mourns him now in his relative anonymity, in his relative fame.

When I enter my parents' home, I see my mother on a chair: wide-eyed, disbelieving, surrounded by neighbors. I rush towards her and hug her. The embrace is weighted with pain. We burst out crying. My mother says, Father wasn't feeling well on Thursday night, he said he had pains in his chest and wanted to go to the hospital. We went to Bikkur Cholim, she continues as we both sob, and I stayed with friends in the neighborhood on the Sabbath so that I could be with him; he was feeling much better. On Saturday night I went home to get him his pajamas and toiletries, she says with barely a voice, and I received a phone call that he had suffered a cardiac arrest. He was gone.

My father is on a stretcher. A small man wrapped in a yellowed, black-trimmed prayer shawl who looks even smaller than he did when he was alive. My father is in the corner, on the other side of the courtyard of the synagogue, on the other side of this world. I can feel his life essence gone. I ask him to forgive me. Now that he is lifeless I ask for it. The rabbi, with a flat voice, recites the prayers for the dead. My mother and I with our blouses rent stand amongst a crowd of mourners and say the prayer, "Blessed are You, Hashem, our God, King of the universe, the true Judge." It is bewildering to say these words after my father has just breathed his last.

My heart is like my father's heart, which broke from too much reality, too many shortages, too many poisoned wells, too long looking after family members with misunderstood illnesses. I think of the last phone call from him a month before he died. Was his singing on the phone about the greatness of God a song of departure? My relationship with my father was not complicated, I loved him and he loved me, but it was not complete. Much was left unsaid. I would have liked him to tell me more about his life, it might have helped him relieve his anguish over the burdens he carried and the losses he suffered while he was still a child: the death of a father and of three brothers in childhood; a trip to Vienna at the age of seventeen, with his mother and an ill sister. He loved this sister and he would wave to her longingly, as she looked out of the hospital ward's window.

My mother is grief-stricken and angry. She says my father was part of her. His sudden heart attack and death tore him away from her body. In a fury she immediately gives all his clothes away. Why him, she asks, there are men who are sick for a long time but are still alive. Only a few days ago we took a walk together, she adds, he was a bit slower than usual, he said he was tired, and I nudged him to walk a little faster.

My mother and I sit shiva. Early in the morning a *minyan* (the quorum of ten men required for communal worship), gather in our house to pray the morning prayers. Friends come to extend their condolences. My parents' friends, members of a tight-knit religious community, bring food. They praise my father for his straightforwardness and his integrity. A true Jerusalemite, they say, quiet, helpful to others, doesn't take interest from those he lends money to, and doesn't pursue them if they don't return it.

In the past, my parents, who religiously visited their ancestors' graves, did not take me to the cemetery for fear of unsettling me. They did not want me to see death or illness. (They were like Buddha's parents, who would not let him, as he was growing up, leave the palace compound for fear he would see people suffer and be in distress.) As a little girl, my parents never took me along to my grandparents' graves on the Mount of Olives in the Old City. Even in my twenties my mother was still concerned about me facing illness and death. Once when I visited her in the hospital, I saw my kindergarten teacher in a wheelchair, her legs amputated. She asked me to rub her back. My mother grew pale for fear that the sight would upset me. Death, to me, was both an ominous and remote event, in the dark, with its back to me, as Rilke would say. I was amazed, once, that the Sephardic women on my street were not ruffled after they had washed a woman's body in preparation for burial.

When in the army my officer called me to his office once, You have received a phone call, you must go home, your aunt died. When I arrived at home my parents looked grim. My mother said, Your father was called to the city morgue to identify your aunt's body; she was hit by a car while crossing the street. I imagined the horror my father felt looking at his sister's crushed body. He couldn't bear articulating what he had seen, how he felt. He said nothing to me.

I returned to the base after a few days. I didn't think much about my dead aunt and my parents. I'd been trained by my parents not to think about such things. Yet, I'd always had a great desire to redeem them of their suffering, to give them pleasure as a way of healing them.

I stay with my mother for a month. A pain in my chest persists the entire time. I sleep on my father's side of my parents' bed. My mother says, Don't you mind sleeping on Father's side? I say, Not at all. My main concern is my mother in her grief, and I think being close to her will mitigate it.

The home is bare without him. My father is no longer at his desk bent over his Talmud, his bookkeeping, his newspaper. I miss his no-nonsense presence, his painstaking efforts to perform domestic chores, fixing a lamp, a handle on the door. He would water the plants—I especially remember the red and yellow leaves of the coleus he cultivated—move them to the terrace at night, and back into the living room during the day. At night, having carefully removed any rubbish from the coffee table, except for the vase and the fake flowers that he would proudly sprinkle with water to get the dust off, my father would take the garbage down.

I remember him on a hot afternoon

> with a bowl of figs by my easy chair,
> his sweet demeanor distilled into a gentle
> gesture of his outstretched hand[2]

He says, I saw these figs, they are very sweet and I knew you would like them. I shrug and say, I don't want any fruit. My father puts the plate down on a table next to me and says with sadness in his eyes, Well, maybe you will want them later. The figs are large and soft, and there are also red grapes and sweet plums on the plate.

My children take their afternoon nap at this time, my mother reads in the living room, which the thick walls keep cool, the city is quiet as I recline on the easy chair with no thought. I shrug off my father's outstretched hand, an act that later makes my heart constrict at the recollection and fills me with regret. Summer afternoons, my father takes my older son, six years old, to his store and lets him help out with chores. He proudly introduces him to his customers. He takes my younger son to the market, and pointing to the offerings, he says, You are a good boy, tell me what you want, anything, and I will buy it for you.

I remember my mother saying, Your father feels inferior because he had no formal education; he could have got a formal education if he only wanted to, but he didn't have the drive. Like Jerusalem, which had been carrying the burden of more than its share, my father, in addition to supporting my mother and me, supported his mother and his two sisters, who were permanent visitors to our house and who led lonely, friendless, unproductive lives. And like the city, loaded with an oppressive past, evident in its weary-laden alleys and streets, my father endured an accumulation of traumas. They made their mark on his determined yet hesitant gait, on the lines around his expressive yet clouded eyes.

He was self-taught. His letters to his customers were eloquent, and his handwriting was beautiful. He liked to read books on archeology and astronomy, books about the universe. He became engrossed with watching the archeological digs in the old city. He often said he hated his store; he waited for the time when he could retire and devote himself to religious studies. Later, when he retired, he joined a Talmud study group. He also volunteered in the maternity ward of a hospital. He wanted to be close to the beginning of life.

Religion gives a taste to life, my father believed. His perception resembled that of John of the Cross, who talked about God in terms of the taste of a fruit. In the new wine of the pomegranates, John of the Cross

173

said, a fruit that signifies a virtue and an attribute of God, the soul that seeks God tastes the delight of God. If I had told that to my father he would have been baffled, intrigued, and ultimately open to the comparison. After all, he may have guessed, "The Song of Songs" must have influenced John of the Cross. In his heart of hearts my father knows that we are all creatures of God, and that being disconnected from Christianity, or from any other racial or religious group, is an artificial way that belongs to narrow-mindedness.

A gap. I imagine what could have been. I envision stroking my father's face, the lines on his face, and soothing him, assuaging his pain. I wish I had talked with him about what ails him, and perhaps about what ails me. He might have offered a quick solution. I don't really know. I never will. Once I wrote him a letter from New York that said I appreciated him giving me room to be myself. Now that he is dead I think about the letter. It feels meager. I could have written more. I search the family album. In a formal photo my father wears a dark suit and a tie, his hat is on a table, a picture of a palm tree in the background. He is twenty-two. He looks steady, fresh, youthful, with a mane of dark hair, and a naïve gaze he would never lose. In another formal photo he is with two men and three women who I imagine are his friends. The men wear suits, the women white blouses and black skirts. They pose seriously, looking straight into the camera. The photo tells me my father, despite his weighty responsibilities at home, had a personal, perhaps even a love life, before he married my mother at the age of twenty-eight.

Two months later my husband and I and our sons, along with my mother, who is in the throes of mourning, celebrate Passover in our home in New York. My sons prepare the house for the holiday as dictated by Jewish law. They meticulously clean every corner. They turn the chairs upside down to remove any hametz that might be hidden there. They empty the pockets of coats in the closets. My mother and I are astonished. We have never seen such zealous conduct. Two days before the Seder, my sons remove every bit of bread, rice, and pasta from the refrigerator and the cabinets, and when Mark is ready for breakfast, he finds the bread and the cereal by the door, ready to be discarded. He quarrels with the kids, knowing—we all know by then—that celebrating

Passover in our home, together with our sons, is something we are not ready for yet.

For a while now, I've been contemplating acquiring skills that would help me become financially independent. Adding a stable income to the little money I make from teaching seminar would, I think, increase my self-respect. I entertain several options, and consult with a couple of my most trusted friends and colleagues. When I ask Louis Simpson about getting an MFA in poetry, he says, That wouldn't give you much, only the option of teaching poetry. Is that what you want to do? Preston says, You could study and teach religion or philosophy in an academic setting. We also discuss psychoanalysis as an option, and he says, I cannot think of anybody who would be better than you, but don't go to a psychoanalytical institute. He doesn't say why, but I learn from other people who have gone through that training that it's torturous and trivial. Preston also suggests doing social work, and that appeals to me. I think it would open up the opportunity to do something I am inclined to do: help people in concrete ways as well as offering them talk therapy.

After a year of study and work in social work, I am assigned to do field work in a hospital hospice unit. The supervisor who interviews me is concerned that my grief over my father's recent death might interfere with my work with patients. I reassure her that my relationship with my father was not complicated, and that my grief is contained. After completing my studies and getting licensed, which was hellish, I get a job working in a hospice unit. Death has become part of my life. It calls me to undo the barriers my parents erected to shield me from its power. I am immersed in treating the dying and their families, and though while doing this work I am plagued with migraines, I plough on. The work involves home care, and takes me to neighborhoods in Manhattan and Brooklyn that I've never been to. I am told that some of the neighborhoods are dangerous, but I ignore this. I travel to the edge of Coney Island, where a patient tells me to watch out for flying bullets, to Bedford-Stuyvesant in Brooklyn, and to Avenues A and B on Manhattan's lower east side. For protection, I carry with me phrases from the Psalms, and I whisper: "God, rescue my soul... for in death there is no remembrance of you," and "How much longer will you hide your face from me?" Some of my patients are ill with AIDS, some with cancer. I talk with them. I pray to be able to help them. They tell me about their lives. They are often angry. Why me? they ask. Some have faith in the next world. Some have regrets. Most are fearful.

Angela and Jessica, who are dying of cancer, are in their thirties. I travel to Brooklyn to see Angela. Her head is bald, her breath heaving. Her emaciated beauty makes me think of Miro's figures, a fish with smooth skin, a leaf in the air. Mysteriously, she keeps a crust of dry bread under her pink pillow. Angela lives with her husband and two children. Does she miss her country, Paraguay, its thickly forested hills and its flowing rivers? Her husband says, What am I going to do after she dies? His anxiety is quiet and contained. Angela talks about the saints she believes in. She hopes for a life to come. But her grief over losing this life is over-powering. Her anguish is contagious. She could have been my daughter, I think. I want to comfort her, lessen her agony. But she is not receptive. She expects something I do not have to give her. She wants her life back. She worries about her severely troubled child. But I also sense a vague relief—soon she will be free of this life and perhaps, her child. After every visit I burst into tears. I have not reached her, helped her. And I am attuned to Rilke,

> How dear you will be to me then, you nights
> of anguish. Why didn't I kneel more deeply to accept you,
> inconsolable sisters, and, surrendering, lose myself
> in your loosened hair. How we squander our hours of pain.
> How we gaze beyond them into the bitter duration
> To see if they have an end[3]

Jessica also lives in Brooklyn, in a pretty brownstone apartment filled with quaint furniture and pictures. She shows me photos of herself before her illness: an attractive, athletic woman with flair. She insists, Why me? She is enraged, and complains about her caregivers, me included. Jessica might have had a better death. If only she could have softened a bit and let some light into her incomprehensible darkness, been receptive to her husband's love and desire for her. If only I could have sweetened her bitterness, companioned her loneliness. After a while she refuses to see me. She would have liked me to be at home in her home, she says, to make myself coffee in her kitchen, to dream with her of vacations. For a few nights I have an aching head, and I wonder how much of my pain is due to *her* pain, and how much to mine, my failure to help her?

I fear failure. I fear not meeting my patients' expectations. I fear not being of help to them. I wonder why my teachers and my supervisors think I am good at what I am doing. Very good, they say. Is it because most of my patients want to continue to see me? Do I expect too much of myself? Do I feel over-responsible? Vanity, I think. If I could only let go of my vanity, I would be more relaxed, more attuned.

There are other terminally ill patients, fearful and perplexed, who are open to speaking about their lives and their dread, to prepare for death. At Eric's request I stretch across his very wide bed and hold his hand. Eric is blinded by AIDS. He tells me about his recurring dream, standing on a desolate street, abandoned. His loneliness is wrenching. But somehow, miraculously, he bears with his blindness and his immense suffering. We form a bond. He feels that I relate to his pain. He wants to know what I look like. He wants me to massage him. Day and night his father sits by the window with a pained expression. He says, I was a king, and now I am nothing. His mother is disbelieving, she is restless, and climbs her son's bed intermittently to take his temperature. When Eric dies I attend the wake. He is dressed in a black suit and his face is made up. I am touched by how still he looks, how restful.

I also form a bond with Sally, my religious patient, who fears her transgressions might prevent her from entering Heaven. It is amazing how tidy she keeps her apartment at this trying time, how neat her nightgowns are, colorful, embroidered at the neckline and hem. After her minister re-baptizes her in the bathtub, at her request, she says, I am ready to meet my maker. At the end of each visit we recite Psalm twenty-three: "Though I pass through a gloomy valley I fear no harm." I wonder about the power of faith, the power of that prayer, the community we form reciting that prayer.

Since my father's death I talk with my mother regularly on the phone.

One summer she visits us at our summer house in Maine. Rainy days. The skies are gray. I pray for my mother to heal. I believe that God is good and merciful, and also, as Whitehead says, that "the beauty of the world, the zest of life, the peace of life, and the mastery of evil"[4] would not achieve actuality but for Him. In this northern village the crows are shrill, disruptive of the peace. I remember the crows in Jerusalem, and don't recall hearing them when flying by our house. Did their cawing become so integral to the sounds of the city that one took them for granted? Other sounds come to mind: the strict, prohibitive, awesome siren, sounding to mark the time for candle-lighting at the beginning of the Sabbath; or the shrieks of the chicken whose body I swung, holding its scrawny legs above my head before Yom Kippur to atone for my sins when I did *Kapparot* (symbolically transferring one's guilt to a fowl), repeating after my parents: "This is my exchange, this is my substitute, this is my atonement." We kept the chickens in a coop on our terrace for about a month, where they became like family to us, before we took them to the slaughterhouse to be slaughtered.

I take my mother for walks. I hope the ocean, the greenery, the blue hills will be of solace to her. My mother, despite her sorrow and loneliness, is able to enjoy the walks.

I think of Rilke's elegy concerning one's own death,

> . . . . . .Murderers are easy
> to understand. But this: that one can contain
> death, the whole of death, even before
> life has begun, can hold it to one's heart
> gently, and not refuse to go on living,
> is inexpressible.[5]

I attend a poetry reading in a church. Two wooden crosses hang on the wall—one with a figure of Jesus, the other draped with a white cloth. The poetry reading is thin. I feel sluggish. I awaken to thoughts about Proust capturing in a short narrative the life of a steeple in Combray: the solitary point slender and pink is seen from one spot, its dark red stones are seen from another, and on a misty autumn morning the steeple is as "a ruin of purple" rising above "the violet thunder-cloud of the vineyard."[6] This northern Maine village is outside the life of striving, and my mother's presence, immersing herself in prayers, is a reminder. My mind wanders to the story about God in Mount Sinai that encapsulates in a few lines of larger-than-life experiences: God coming down on the mountain in the form of fire, smoke streaming and trumpets sounding; blessings and curses, and the commandment to wash one's clothes in preparation for receiving the Ten Commandments, are clearly heard.

I become aware that the religious rules I think are meaningless and rigid can be a tool for getting closer to God. The awareness takes a while, a long while; it comes mainly through watching my sons practice the religion. The cleaning and scrubbing before Passover, and the other innumerable religious rules, whether they involve the Sabbath, or the prayers, or the holidays, are opportunities, as I further realize, to pause and contemplate. The meticulous ordering of the Seder table and the reading of the Haggadah—in remembrance of the liberation of the Jews from Egypt—can be a setting for transcendence, and applied to personal freedom.

To my delight, I learn that my sons' religious practice, which I consider strict, is also flexible. When they show me the places in the prayer book where one can insert personal prayers I feel relief. Sometimes I hold the prayer book next to my chest. I look out of the window at the vastness, the river, the miracle of it all. A red-tailed hawk perches on the upper branches of a tree across from our window. Squirrels swiftly climb the trees; clouds pass detachedly. I am free to make the traditional prayers my own.

My husband, who was raised in a Reform Jewish home and who grew up feeling frightened by being Jewish in a non-Jewish world, is shocked by the path our sons have chosen. His grammar school had very few Jews, and his best friend was a Greek Orthodox boy whose house was a second home to him and whose parents celebrated Christmas and Easter with zest. Mark's parents and the rest of the Reform Jewish community were striving to live "the American Way." And the American way was the gentile way.

Mark had been running away from Judaism. He associated his grandfather's synagogue, which he visited on Yom Kippur—a small room
glaringly "old country," a group of men speaking Yiddish—with anti-
Semitism, and the persecution of Jews in the past. The synagogue spoke
of impoverishment, the air was stuffy, the smell stale. Mark believed
that if Jews remained that way, they would be annihilated. He saw the
people who gathered in the Reform synagogue his parents attended as
hypocritical. Their attendance amounted to a social event. There was
nothing in their conduct or in their thinking, or in the atmosphere in
the temple that embodied an attempt to get closer to God. And Sunday
school was empty of serious content and discipline. It gave Mark and his
friends a chance to misbehave. He was convinced the practice of Judaism
was nothing but anachronistic when Ultra-Orthodox, superficial and
hypocritical when Reform. That his own sons would choose to practice a
religion in a way that would deprive them of the best of culture, education, and the knowledge of other great religions, saddens him.

I discuss with Mark the freedom our sons need to exercise in choosing
their paths. We remind ourselves that we too chose paths contrary to
our parents' expectations, and perhaps they take after us: I turned away
from being religiously observant and left the country, the latter causing
my mother to be depressed for several years. Mark became an artist,
rebelling against doing anything that smacked of business or academia,
displeasing especially his father, who couldn't see the making of art as
justified or necessary unless one was a Picasso who enjoyed fame and
was able to sell his art.

I consider the freedom to live my own life and the freedom for all to live
their own lives sacred territory, and I cannot envision, without suffering
pangs of conscience, being critical of or negating anyone's choices, no
matter how strange or different their ways may be from mine. The difference in the extent to which Mark and I accept and tolerate our sons' new
way of life, creates heated debates and fights between us, and between
him and our children. There are periods in which we go on battling
with each other, on and on, until we look at ourselves, and realize our
self-righteousness. Reconciliations are warm. We get closer to each other

and to our sons—who, my husband and I agree—are practicing a costly Judaism, following the law and what is best in it: compassion, humanness, sincerity.

I remember when my younger son was nine years old, I asked him why he thought the Jews survived. Because they want to, he answered. I think of him now, on this Eve of Rosh Hashanah, he too must dip the apple in honey. I think of him returning from the synagogue at the end of the Sabbath, carefully attending to every detail of the ritual. He lights the multi-wick candle his young son is holding. He blesses God for creating the fruit of the vine and the illuminations of the fire, he says the prayer deliberately as he holds a cup of wine and the different fragrant spices. Then he sits for a while: he pauses to recite the prayers that guard the holy as the Sabbath departs. He sits for a long while reciting the prayers.

Around Christmas and New Year's, when everything in New York is glitter and celebration, I think with sadness of my younger son leaving behind his beloved city—its architecture, museums, and galleries; its avenues, like West End, which to him has a mysterious dark quality, yet opens up to a light at the horizon. Rain and cold never deter him from taking long walks in the city's streets and its parks. I think of his understanding of art, his knowledge of the labyrinthine Metropolitan Museum of Art.

My older son turns to blessings and prayer as a young adult. He prays the morning prayers my father had showed him in the prayer book, starting with "May your Name be praised forever." He says these prayers with devotion. When he turns to adhere to the full practice of religion and has a family, the festival of Passover is pivotal to him. The destruction of hametz becomes a transcendental rite to dismiss impurities from the heart. He makes puppet shows for his children in which the stories of the Haggadah are retold with new meanings, personal meanings.

Sometimes I grieve about my older son retreating from the culture he so loved: William Hoffman's wrenching play As Is, the musical Sweeney Todd. He withdrew from the delight he took in the humorous TV shows—*I Love Lucy* and *The Honeymooners*, and the dissonant sculptures of Ebers he collected. He loved to listen to the sensual songs of Edith Piaf, watch the alluring persona of Marlene Dietrich. A poster by Niki de Saint Phalle hung in his room was a favorite.

One spring my husband and I attend a Seder in Jerusalem at his house. As I cuddle my grandchildren dressed in their new clothes for the holiday, enjoying the energy this new family exudes—a creativity within the traditional rites—something in me lifts: an unyielding regret I've had about not having recognized in the past my son's creativity, his clay work—the beautiful, quirky ceramic vase—and the poignant photographs he made as a youngster. Life is larger than the past, I think. Here, around the Seder table, there is fullness, plentitude, a transcendence of everything temporal.

16

UNDER CLUSTERS OF GREEN GRAPES

For a while now, I've become interested in ideas about what can be done to help resolve the Israeli/Palestinian conflict. I read philosophy books. Fresh ideas flood my mind. I cut articles from newspapers that report on acts of kindness between Israelis and Palestinians. I search religious sources for hints about concessions for the sake of peace. Deep inside me I hear my father's voice speaking Arabic with his Arab customers. I can see him in his store doing business with them. I too want to get close to the Palestinians and speak their language.

Mark, who is interested in the conflict as well, believes that the two peoples don't see each other as real, life-sized. In 1999 he originates a photographic project that involves young Israeli-Arabs and Jews photographing each other and their surroundings. The goal of the project is to lessen the prejudices and better the attitudes of Jews and Arabs towards each other. Matnassim, The Israel Association of Community Centers, is prepared to sponsor and organize the project. They arrange meetings with people who are members of the centers throughout the country. Mark asks me to assist him on many of his trips by conducting interviews with the participants. For years now, Mark and I have worked together sporadically. I have been working with him and Kathie, on and off, on putting together Preston's teachings into a book, a daunting undertaking, which we haven't consistently pursued. But when we do work together, the work goes well, as each of us brings a particular strength to the collaborative project. Over the years Mark asked me to help him with a number of photographic projects that involved interviewing the subjects he photographed. I accommodated him with good results. Interviewing is a skill that comes naturally to me, coupled with my years of experience of doing interviews on the radio, with patients, and with seminar students. Helping Mark with this project, however, is different. I am thrilled by the opportunity to do interviews in my home country, meeting Arabs and interviewing them in their own environment.

The first Arabs I meet, associated with Matnassim, are in Kamana, a Bedouin village in Western Galilee. Miri, a young Jewish woman and a member of the center in the village Yodfat, volunteers to join us as part of the project. Our car climbs the dirt road leading to the mountaintop village. There are trees and greenery in the Beit Hakerem Valley below, but as we get closer to the village, a rocky soil, and an almost bare terrain scattered with boulders and with only a few trees, emerge. I have the strange feeling of having landed in an uninhabitable place. It is as if the village had no foundation. Lonely and vulnerable, it stands below a blue sky, with no recourse to the outside world. The houses on its outskirts are made of cinder blocks and corrugated metal; the telephone and electrical wires are connected chaotically from pole to pole, house to house. In the back of most of the houses are animal pens strewn with debris.

Mark and I visit with Ali, a school supervisor who hosts us under clusters of grapes hanging from slender vines supported by wooden slats. The thatch we sit in is intimate like a sealed spring, with plentiful delectable green grapes resplendent in the sun that streaks through. Nearby is a shed in which a woman, wearing a long heavy dress and a head covering, is baking pita bread. The shed is windowless. With easy-flowing movements she places a tray of dough in the oven. I can see the flames through the oven's opening. I go in the shed but it is intolerably hot. I step outside and keep looking in. She smiles. Bread-making is a habit for her. She displays a flair for it. Ali serves us the bread, warm and generous, with labane and olives.

For the project I record Ali's story about the life of his Bedouin tribe. His ancestors fled Syria to escape paying taxes to the Turks, and settled on the mountain they now inhabit, naming their village Kamana. As a child Ali walked eight kilometers to school. On rainy days, without proper clothes and shoes, he would arrive at school wet and muddy. The other Arab kids who came from peasant families shunned him. He was dirty, they said. Now he dresses neatly in a white shirt and dark pants, his hair is combed carefully, and his manner is urban.

From the mountain we see the valley shimmering, the wind is hard but friendly. Three cows are kept in an open shed, a watchdog barks at us. We, the Bedouins, says Ali, don't advance because we don't ask for anything; we are shy people. I think of how Ali and I are similar in our aspirations. Although Ali's circumstances and mine are different—he lives among the poor, and I among the affluent—we share a similar struggle to make our lives better.

Miri, Mark, and I walk to Nadia's house to photograph and interview her. Nadia is a young woman and a member of the center. Her face is pallid, her lips have a touch of lipstick. She is dressed like most of the young women in the village, in jeans and a tee shirt, unlike the old women who wear long dresses. She is delighted to see us and comes forward to welcome us heartily, suggesting that our visit is an adventure for her, a diversion from her repetitive life. Her house sits on the top of the mountain, and even as the sun shines and the sky is clear, a wind is brewing on all sides. Nadia's father was killed in an automobile accident twenty years ago, the first day on his job. Nadia's mother has since cloaked herself in stiff grief. Yet today she smiles. She wants us to eat at her house. She is happy to host us. We linger. I wonder whether her garden, where the tall squash flowers grow, comforts her. I savor the sight of the grapevines that protect her garden from the sun and gaze at the dry weeds and the few dusty trees along her unpaved path. I think of how she is resigned to her widowed life, and of her three unmarried daughters with their thin, vulnerable bodies, bereft of a father who would, if alive, spare them of the twenty long years of sadness that aggrieves their gentle faces.

We continue to walk. Several men sit under almond trees. They invite us to sit with them. We are served coffee, coffee brewed for hours, black and bitter, thick like earth. The sea-green almonds humbly hanging from delicate branches remind me of the hard and raw almonds I used to eat as a child, plucked from a tree in an uncultivated field. We ate them with a pinch of salt, unwashed, imagining ourselves true and as tough as the almonds. The men sit aimlessly, perhaps dreaming of an adventurous nomadic existence. This is leisure, I think. Perhaps this ambiance is a remnant of life in the desert, life in tents, a direct contact with everything raw and natural and unsullied. The man next to me has a diseased half-shut eye, some of his teeth are missing, some are discolored, yet when he smiles a spark in his one good blue eye lights up and for a moment he looks like Paul Newman. He tells me about his longings for wandering, the desert, life without constraints. He tells me about the wedding tomorrow, with drums and singing, feasting on lamb now being sliced on a big table to be cooked tomorrow before the wedding, and the hundreds of people who will come from the villages around, to feast, to dance, to sing. The man tells me about his sons and his wife as the afternoon begins to fade and the sun weakens. His half-shut eye tires, it is almost completely shut. I like his expressions of longings for a past of wanderings that he hasn't personally experienced but that was related to him as family history. The longings match my own, for something in my past that is familiar, which I belong to in body and in blood, something uniquely Mid-Eastern, an Arabic song blasting from my Sephardic neighbor's radio, fresh tomatoes in the Arab market, a natural environment of raw almonds in almost deserted fields and in the impoverished gardens of those less fortunate than the people I generally associate with today.

In the eyes of many Israelis, neither Ali nor the man with the half-shut eye typifies the Arabs. Ammar did. Ammar who did manual labor. He was uneducated, from one of the Arab villages surrounding Jerusalem. Ammar used to clean my parents' house. My parents were pleased with the job he did, and they recommended him to their neighbors. Soon he was in demand, cleaning Jewish homes in their neighborhood. He was punctual, his work was thorough, and he was trustworthy. It was rumored he bought a house with the money he made from house cleaning. It was also rumored that one of his sons is a terrorist, wounded in a terror attack against Israel.

In the days of my growing up, we Sabras had contempt for the Arabs. We felt no compunction for being dismissive of them. We saw them as primitive; we belittled them for not making progress in areas we excelled in, agriculture and trade and education, and for the way they treated their women, keeping them unseen in the back of their houses when visitors came. They were not idealistic nor were they industrious. Since they lost the Independence War we saw them as losers. In our eyes they were just fellahin, primitive peasants, who lived in disorganized villages, some whiling away their time in cafés smoking narghiles. No one told us of their intellectual accomplishments, their generosity, their entrepreneurial acumen. They were less than us. Immersed in our idealism, our aspirations and songs, we ignored the undercurrent of resentment they felt towards us. We proudly sang about the land, our land, the song of a young girl with a bunch of anemones, the song about pioneers planting a field in Tel Hai, the song about making the desert bloom, the song about a pomegranate tree whose scent spreads between Jericho and the Dead Sea. We didn't entertain the thought that the Palestinians born on this land might share with us a hardy spirit, the distinctive attribute of the native fruit Sabra, sweet inside and prickly outside. We dismissed any notion of equality between us. But on this visit to Arab villages and towns the perception of the Arabs as primitive begins to fade.

In Umm el-Fahm we meet Ayman, who hosts my husband and me. Ayman is a poet. He is intelligent and intellectually honest. I reflect upon the meaning of the handwritten dedication in the book of his poems he gives us, which says, "Scattered—please/ Do not gather me." Does Ayman talk about a personal scattering, a cultural or a political one? Is the phrase a translation of one of his poem in Arabic? I neglect to ask, and I regret that I had not kept practicing the Arabic I learned in school. Some of Ayman's poems were translated into Hebrew by an Israeli Jew, though his Hebrew is just as good as that of any Jew.

Ayman says, I was my grandmother's shoes. As she aged her eyesight failed and I helped her go wherever she wanted. He shows Mark and me her grave on the small hill across the street from where we stand. We visit Ayman's former school, the building and the courtyard. The sinks in the courtyard are primitive. He says, The school has always been poor; the Israelis don't give us enough money for schools. Once I went to Bethlehem, he says, and the Israelis stopped me, but a friend of mine, a Druze, who was stationed there, acknowledged me, and they let me go without interrogating me. I was very humiliated when they stopped me, he adds.

I think of the land, the tradition of toil, life on mountains, distress under foreign occupations, the religious secrets of the Druze, the Sufis merging with a higher spirit. I think of Rumi's poetry, the "innermost chambers."

These orchards, says Ayman, pointing to the trees as we stand on a mountain, belonged to my grandfather, then he divided them between his sons. I look across the landscape. The wind is unforgiving, raising dust. Were these trees a paradise once? Ayman and I belong to this land, the trees, the stones. I want nothing else but to continue to stand here. I want nothing else but that others, Israelis and Palestinians, will feel the kinship I suddenly feel with Ayman and the Palestinians. And that the natural tie, buried below the political hostilities, will strengthen, grow, and blossom.

Is the center of Umm el-Fahm, where we now walk, with its crammed houses, narrow, steep streets, and dense, defiant mood, also a paradise lost? Israeli Jews see Umm as a volatile town, uncompromising, a fifth column. Two Arab youths sit on a low wall. There is nothing here, they say. They look into a void, then suspiciously at us. But we feel protected by Ayman, a husky man, self-possessed, a poet, a non-practicing Muslim, from a prominent local family. Ayman tells me there are many political groups in Umm el-Fahm. Communists too? Yes, he says.

The call from the minaret accompanies our walk. The man is singing prayers, I say. Ayman laughs, You don't sing prayers, you recite them. But to me this town is also a song; cheerful voices of children, and smiles of Arabs who stand behind counters of fresh nuts and crates of vegetables, and the amiable barber whom we visit and who befriends us. The essential things about religion are self-improvement and humility, says Ayman. I am drawn to Ayman, his understanding. I am excited about sharing ideas with him.

Most evenings, Ayman, his friends and cousins, meet in the barbershop to talk. An old tradition. The barber, "the talker," who hears everything, passes on to them what he hears.

At Ayman's home the hospitality is unreserved. Ayman's mother, with her classical features, welcomes us with an erect posture, an open, unstudied smile. Genuinely warm, somewhat weary, and proud of her erudite children, she serves us Coca-Cola, watermelon, nuts, and coffee. She complains about Jewish residents of a neighborhood in a northern town who will not permit her daughter and her husband to live there as neighbors.

I sink into a chair and listen with rapt attention to Ayman reading his poetry. I think of the desert, the wanderings, the adventure of the tent. The desert is miles away. Years away. Receding into oblivion. Did I hear the word blood? Whose blood? Arabs' spilled by Jews? I think of the gentle spirit of the mint garden we saw this morning, and how it shook in the harsh wind.

While traveling to meetings with participants in the project, I enjoy the landscape, round hills, olive and oak trees, white almond blossoms. Along the way to Daliyat el-Carmel, before Mark and I stop for a short visit in Isfiya, I see a hawk motionless in the air, cyclamen among rocks, delicate leaves on trees. Isfiya, a Druze village with quiet streets and content shops, takes in the silence of Heaven. I think of the servants of God in the Jewish morning prayers, exclaiming "Holy, Holy." And I imagine the Druze priest from Isfiya saying "Holy, Holy." We meet Yusuf, the young Druze composer, and I think of him blessing Western and Eastern music, blessing the Druze tradition which one mustn't offend, blessing the natural world, the pines and cypresses surrounding his village, the wild cows, the thorns. He blesses his father, the author, his mother who plants trees, enduringly, to fight her illness with spiritual strength.

We go by "The Bakery of Blessings," and I think of the power of blessings. Blessings to pass on from one generation to another, blessings before you eat bread and after, blessings of the Druze priest who remembers Jethro and Moses at the threshold of the desert, blessings when you meet the Muslim Arab, blessings when you meet the Druze, blessing their longings, their sadness and joy. And you bless God who made the rooster to distinguish between day and night, and made me a woman to distinguish between falsity and truth, to distinguish between the real Druze and the Druze of my ignorant mind. And I repent my prejudice, the sin of sloth, my broken thoughts.

We arrive in Daliyat. And I bless Daliyat in the hushed mountains; bless the tribe, bless the *hamula* (extended family living in proximity to each other), the secrets of the religion. And I bless my mother who accepts all souls. And I bless my father who took me to visit the Temple Mount after the war in 1967.

We walk by the sea in Akko. I think of Akko's past, the ships, the victories, the defeat of the biblical Asher and Yanai. The sea moves away like a dreamy sail. It is solitary, monastic, inviolate. The waves flatten, glass-smooth, horizons stretched. An egret dips its beak in the water. Fishermen stand on the shore with long lines. A bride is in white, her bridegroom in black. The photographer instructs the bride to look at the sea, then to look at her man.

In the harbor of Akko debris, faint hope. Arab youths sit on benches, unemployed. We enter a restaurant and eat broiled fish sprinkled with lemon juice. We take a walk. We see parts of ancient engravings on walls, the grandiose structures of al-Jezzar that endures like memory. By the sea is a statue of an imprisoned Jewish underground fighter boring a hole in the prison wall. And I can see a Jewish prisoner led to be hanged by the British authorities, his face young, bewildered, brave.

The youth center in Akko was once a palace. Light-green walls emit a light. Ceiling is high. Turkish coffee is served, heavy like summer leaves. Arab and Jewish youths gather. They photograph each other. I record them talking with each other. The counselor talks about Dervish dancing, the dance he once danced, the way he circled around Jerusalem, twirling around Jerusalem without inhibition. And I think of the unity of the Sufi poet Rumi and his mentor Sham. We meet Nur, a beautiful, young, and zestful Muslim. She takes us up to a roof of a house to show us the towers, the mosques. She photographs a rusty pipe. She wants to make her yearnings into art. She takes us for a walk by the wall, in dark and empty alleys. I feel the strength beneath the emptiness, beneath the dull wall.

After completing his work in the north Mark and I travel to Beit Safafa, an Arab enclave in Jerusalem, to continue working on his project. When I was growing up I would see Beit Safafa from afar, remote and unapproachable, pondering its fate, a jumble of electrical lines rising above its hills like warning signs. Beit Safafa evoked in me a sense of danger. In the north of Jerusalem, where I lived, the neighborhoods were plain to me. I knew the names of most streets—their length and breadth, the flat parts, and where they turned hilly. I knew where the "good" streets were—it was where I wanted to live. But the very southern parts of the city were distant and strange, especially the Arab neighborhoods. After the Independence War the railroad tracks divided Beit Safafa into two, one half was ruled by Jordan, the other by Israel. I thought the people of the village were like fugitives with the sign of Cain marked on their foreheads. They were made to look, in my mind, like the impure who were commanded to stay outside the Israelite camp in the desert.

Beit Safafa is now united under Israeli rule. Under a white and sad sky the narrow, quiet streets intertwine, railroad tracks are abandoned. A group of Jewish women and a group of Arab women gather in a room with small windows. Amal, an Arab woman, is stateless. In her passport the space for a state is blank. She tells me that whenever she wants to go abroad she has to go to Jordan, get her passport stamped there. The Israelis don't want us to become Israeli citizens, she says bitterly. (A Jewish woman from the nearby Jewish neighborhood Gonnen tells me later that it is not true, and that the people from Beit Safafa are the ones who don't want to become Israeli citizens.) Lana, an Arab woman whose son was killed in an Intifada, puts her arm around me and grips my shoulder with a sorrow that belongs only to a bereaved mother, a sorrow that surrounded the house across the street from my parents' house that belonged to a family who lost two sons in the war of 1948.

In this airless room with minimal decorations, in a house made of white stone, we women are reticent, waiting, until one begins to talk about Farid el-Atrache, the Egyptian singer, and another responds with enthusiasm, and then another begins to sing a song of his, and soon the two groups, the Arab and the Jewish, are both singing the song together.

17

MOTHER AND MOTHERLAND

At the onset of the second intifada in 2000, I hear on the news that a riot began after Palestinians throw stones at Israeli soldiers. The soldiers shoot back. In Ramallah, a Palestinian mob lynches two Israeli soldiers: The mob throws one Israeli soldier out of a window into a crowd that stomps on him, gouges his eyes. I pray, "May His great Name grow exalted and sanctified."

Ramallah. The sound once rolled like the gentle slopes surrounding the town. In 1945, before the Independence War, an Arab customer of my father who lived in Ramallah once invited our family for a visit. The bus, small, unsturdy, its color fading, unlike the well-painted, well-built Jewish buses, belonged to an Arab company, and commuted only between Arab villages and towns. When my parents and I sat on the bus I felt a strange excitement. I felt privileged. None of my friends ever visited people in an Arab town, and none of their parents could relate to Arabs with the ease my father did.

We passed a number of Arab villages. Except for a few scattered olive trees and small squarish houses, the land was bare but with its own soft beauty, lying in a warm and carefree slumber. A strong light unfolded as the bus went by, a light stronger than rites and laws. At each stop my heart leapt. I craved to leave the bus and run in those thorny yellow fields. To enter those Arab homes. Perhaps stay there a while. I was sitting next to my mother, who wore a green summer dress to complement her reddish hair and fair skin. My father was chatting with some Arabs. He was pleased to demonstrate his fluency in Arabic. He would later tell me of the Arabs' flair for flattery, and how they would praise the beauty of my mother.

When we arrived in Ramallah, the hills and houses were tinged with deep blue. I thought of Abraham and Sara and how they greeted the three angels disguised as travelers. Now we were the visiting angels, and our hosts were Abraham and Sara, who upon meeting us showered us with greetings. My parents spent the afternoon chatting with our hosts on the terrace, while I ran around in circles with their children, their faces lit with friendliness.

In 2001 the intifada escalates. I think of the Arabs' riots in 1929 and 1936, and of Hajj Amin al-Hussenie, the Mufti of Jerusalem, who embodied the hatred towards the Jews, and whose name for a long time sent shivers down our spines. And I recall Ma'arri, a Muslim poet and free thinker born in the tenth century who said,

> 'Tis sadness enough that all the righteous are gone together and that we are left alone to inhabit the earth.
> Truly, for a long while Iráq and Syria have been two ciphers: the king's power in them is an empty name.
> The people are ruled by devils invested with absolute authority: in every land there is a devil in the shape of a governor—
> One who does not care though all the folk starve, if he can pass the night drinking wine with his belly full.[1]

That year on September 11th two American planes carrying hundreds of civilian passengers are hijacked by Arab suicide bombers who fly the planes into the Twin Towers in New York. Three thousand people die. Some, to escape the blasting fires, jump from the upper-story windows, others are trapped on the roof, and others die when the buildings implode. New Yorkers are dumbfounded. The world is shocked. America feels a grief it hasn't known for decades. My friends in Israel call me to express their shock and their sympathy. We know how terrible people in New York feel, they say, we know what it's like to be attacked unexpectedly, and in unexpected ways; maybe now the world will understand us.

Also that year, a U.N. conference on racism takes place in South Africa. A Palestinian group plans to issue a statement equating Zionism with racism. It accuses Israel of genocide. It has convened to redress harm, but what echoes in me are the words of the Spanish poet Blas de Otero, who said, in a different context, that these were great steps backward, toward the giant night of the cliffs.

These attacks make me feel distraught. I want to tell about Israelis' need to claim sanctuary in a land they have been longing for, and fortify it against persecution for the entire Jewish people. I want to express my own longing for my Motherland, saying, All I want, all I need, is nothing so much as a slope of Bab-el-Wad—the *wadi* (a valley) on the way to Jerusalem—for my soul to inhabit, a small strip of it, a tiny patch of its earth. I picture myself standing with my back against dark cliffs, singled out and targeted by a firing squad for keeping intact the memory of Bab-el-Wad—where convoys to Jerusalem passed through during the siege of the city in 1948—stringing together ancient remembrances of the wadi with my present life, and singing Haim Guri's old song about the wadi, where sadness and majesty and a burnt armored truck and a name of an unknown dwelt together.

Jericho, an Arab town that once waved an olive branch, is suddenly swept by terror. Arabs shoot at Israeli soldiers. Israeli soldiers shoot at Palestinians and shell Palestinian buildings. I can see the towering palm trees quiver above a group of Arabs in a small café, and I write,

> Gentle Jericho.
> I loved your spring
> I visited once
> as a little girl.
>
> Then I believed the purging power
> of springs.
> Your slow trickle of water
> was a kiss
> to brush my face against. . . .
>
> And I believe again.
> In your spacious cafés.
> Cool, hospitable ceilings.
> In your gesture
> yet undeciphered.

Like a lover
I seek you
among the grape-
vines.
Forever unpossessive
I thirst
for your hard-seeded
intimate
fruit.[2]

I would like to go to Jericho and rinse my face with the wholesome water
of Elisha's Spring. I would like to sit by that spring and dream of the
angel of God who said to the tearful Hagar that he would make her son
into a great nation. Sitting by that spring I will dream of Esau who wept
and begged his father for a blessing after finding out that his brother
Jacob had fraudulently taken his. And I think of the compassion my
ancestor Reb Shmelke from Nikolsburg, a Hasid master, had for Esau, a
declared enemy. He referred to the Midrash that says the Messiah will
not come before the tears of Esau have ceased to flow, and remarked that
the tears of Esau "are the tears which all human beings weep when they
ask something for themselves. . ."[3]

They say it is too early to dream of two nations living side by side. They
say the call for peace is as faint-sounding as a lone bird's on a roof. But
sitting by the spring, whose bitter water once killed the unborn, I will
dream of the Arab with his goat in the field by my childhood house,

A she-goat, soft face,
next to an Arab man in the barren field. . . .

The woman, smiling, hands over the pot to the Arab.
He takes it gently and milks the goat.
He hands the pot back to her,
and she puts a coin in his hand—
a quiet transaction, like an omen of an ancient covenant,
when trading was a great solid promise.[4]

I will dream of my father's Arab customer from before the War of Independence, who arranged to pay a debt to my father through enemy lines. It is too early, they say. And yet sitting by the spring that had turned sweet I will dream of the angel who had pity on Hagar and Ishmael in the desert. I hear the muezzin calling for war, and I see the burning of Israeli flags in Gaza, and the expressions of hate, resistance, and defiance on Palestinian faces. And I imagine a wound festering on the center of their disaffected faces, a wound decades old, beginning at the turn of the twentieth century, that slowly developed and festered. And I will dream of Ishmael, saved by the angel of God, then going his own way and building his own great nation. And I will dream of Ephraim and Menashe growing and increasing, and I will dream of palm trees standing tall, seaports thriving, and the land, the desired land, blessed with grain and flowers, and ancient mountains rising.

There are already signs of hunger in Hebron. And I think of my mother in her small town in Poland, hungry for bread when she came home from school, and of her mother who had gone to another town for medical treatment, and how sometimes she would go to a relative's home and eat a potato. And I think of the people in Deheisheh, the Palestinian refugee camp, who think every day is their last. I have never been to Deheisheh, but I read the online diary of a journalist who is there and I picture scarcity of food, and scarcity of water, and scarcity of beds and roofs, and I imagine scarcity of thought, and scarcity of life—real life, aliveness.

I am far away from Deheisheh, from Jerusalem, from my mother. I am far away from the ills that grip my country and the weakening condition of my mother. I am far away from home.

I am immersed in seminar teaching, and in writing poetry and essays. In addition to working together to transcribe Preston's tapes, Kathie and I write interdisciplinary essays in which there is a confluence of Preston's philosophical way of thinking and our own ideas from seminar readings. In a psychoanalytical session Preston once said to me, You and Kathie are in my direct apostolic succession. Kathie was a math teacher, and is a writer and editor of math textbooks. We met in Preston's seminar and have been friends for years. We understand each other, and complement each other. Kathie's reading is close, she is quick to understand, and she inspires me with not letting go until she fully comprehends an idea. I bring to the partnership my ability to contain and mull over chaos of ideas, and to tolerate paradoxes. Our emphasis is on the spiritual life. We preserve Preston's tone of mind, appealing to truth and rejecting dogmatic finality. Kathie's Protestantism and my Judaism contribute to the multiplicity of our resources. Several of our essays are published. *The Journal of Religion and Health* has published a couple of them, and its editor, Barry Ulanov, tells us that he will teach our essay "Thoughts on Psyche, Soul, and Spirit" in his class at the Union Theological Seminary. Our article on Milarepa and his demons as aids to spiritual growth is also published, and another, discussing creative advance in Jeremiah, is published *in Eretz Acheret* in Jerusalem. Our article "The Israeli/ Palestinian Conflict: A New Beginning," appears in the online version of *Tikkun* magazine, and "Subtleties of the Spirit" appears online and in hard copy in *Miranda Literary Magazine*.

For a while Sara and I study Talmud with a rabbi in one of the west side synagogues, and I continue to attend my synagogue on the Sabbath and on the holidays. Mark rarely joins me, but he wholeheartedly supports my going there. On Sabbath mornings when I debate with myself whether to go, he warmly encourages me, Why won't you go? You get so much out of it. His encouragement delights me. He is pleased with the way I practice Judaism, Not blindly, he says, You know a lot about religion, and you are not buying the whole package. You are critical of parts of the practice.

In the early years of the new millennium, when Israel is gripped by terror, and my mother is weak, I must leave my work and go to Jerusalem. I ought not to be separated from my mother, and the streets in Jerusalem, which are empty at night, and from my friends who are afraid. I ought to be close to the mountains and gates around Jerusalem, the walls that unite and separate, the ravens, the black ravens perching in the few trees on the street where I grew up, the monastery in the Valley of the Cross, neglected and dirty inside where we did our pre-army training; the vast valley that surrounded the fortress, blooming with flowers in spring.

I ought not to be separated from the beggars at the Wailing Wall who pull at your dress, and with a mournful and fretful tone plead with you to give them *tzddakah* (charity), promising a future with plenty of blessings. I ought to cite the Psalms at the Wailing Wall: "God whom I praise, / break your silence."

I ought to be with my mother. Like Camus' character Jean, I have been faithful to her. I never betrayed her. Though very demanding of me, my mother, for her part, has always been on my side. Had I murdered someone she would be on my side.

I read William Blake. I want to oppose obedience, to oppose restraint; to be free of consistencies; to tolerate contraries, to be able to move from ruth to ruthlessness, from ruthlessness to ruth, dream simultaneously of an undivided Jerusalem and of a divided Jerusalem. I want to participate in Blake's celebration of life. And yet, I say to myself again, I ought to be in Jerusalem, I ought to be with my mother.

I travel to Jerusalem. I visit my mother. I have begun calling the land of Israel "Motherland"—a tie that will not be unloosened, despite distance, despite forgetfulness. There are deaths in Jerusalem, Ramallah, and at Joseph's tomb. My mother, now 90 years old, suffers pain. She is sitting on her bed, thin, small, with a fractured shoulder. The land is fragmented. My mother is looking out her window, comforted by leaves that tremble in the breeze. It is hot, she says, but there is a light movement in the trees. The intifada and the suicide bombing continue. There are guards who check your bags at cafés and restaurants and hotels. In malls you go through metal detectors. You look for suspicious objects and suspicious people wherever you are.

I ask myself, Will time heal? Will my mother heal? Will time reveal salvation, or will it disclose destruction? Will the Jews' appeal to the past, the belief that God will ultimately fulfill His promise to His chosen people, continue to be endorsed by people in Israel?

When we were growing up we did not think that years later Jerusalem would be a city of strife. That there would be hard struggles for the land, invasions, killings, occupations. I did not imagine that Gabriel, a relative's son, would be killed on the Lebanese border. I did not think that I would witness his father watering devoutly a small garden every morning, a garden he would erect in his son's memory, and that evenings, on the way home from the synagogue, he would take a detour, walking on small, dark streets. He does not want to see anyone. And he does not want anyone to see him. He feels shame. He has been diminished by the loss of his son. By this complete loss.

We did not foresee that terror and deaths would shatter the rocky soil in the north, that Israel would invade, and that Arabs would terrorize, celebrate terror; that within the terror, a murmur, a still-wistful voice, would rise like a sliver of moon, like the prayer of Hannah it would rise, a tremor of lips, inaudible like the heart, the heart itself, from among the changing of flags, the rhetoric, the propaganda; that a small, nostalgic voice of a Jewish mother who had lost her son on the Lebanese border would be heard and would become like the sound of Jonah from the belly of the fish, Jonah calling from the heart of the sea, a call in distress, resounding like the wailing siren of Remembrance Day that brings the nation to a standstill. And that an Arab woman will return to her Lebanese village and will sit in her garden among the rubble, and will see the tree in her garden she hasn't seen for years, sits in the shade of her tree that like Jonah's tree had blossomed, then withered, at night.

Upon coming back to New York, after spending three weeks in Jerusalem, I walk on 79th Street, and see American flags hanging from windows, above shops, everywhere. It is six weeks after 9/11. I think, What are American flags doing in Jerusalem? I wonder about it for a minute or two, and then suddenly I realize that I am back in New York. For a short time I am a native of both Jerusalem and New York. I live in two cities. I feel an affinity with the unyielding blue-and-white Israeli flag, and with the Star-Spangled American banner, the bold red, white, and blue. I feel an affinity with America I have not felt before.

18

THE TERRACE THAT BASKED IN THE SUNLIGHT

On my next trip to Jerusalem I visit the neighborhood I grew up in. I linger on the street that descends from the market to where I used to live, and I pass by the white corner building with the round terrace, unusual given the neighborhood's mostly square architecture, and the grocery store beneath it, which I enjoy recalling while in New York. The street has remained the same: poorly paved, with narrow sidewalks. Lacking the breadth and diversity of the grand streets in New York, it offers a comforting, homelike intimacy, a reassuring simplicity. The field nearby is moist, green, and thorny, an indestructible foundation.

Jerusalem is my foundation. And yet if I had stayed in Jerusalem I would have lamented with Cavafy: "What trouble, what a burden small cities are—what lack of freedom."[1] Like him, I would have felt that I need a large city to roam and to wander in the streets, to visit the many museums and to contemplate paintings by Van Gogh, Rembrandt, de Kooning, Jasper Johns, to absorb the energy the city exudes, to be in touch with different cultures and people that give us truth and beauty and opportunities to learn about the other. To watch parents relating to their children on the subway. To observe a child, restless and excited, watching from the window the trains going by; a woman meticulously putting makeup on; tourists studying a map; street singers, a capella singers, beggars—all looking for handouts; a homeless, toothless beggar who kneels and sings to me that he has been waiting for me all of his life.

It is 2003. The population in my old neighborhood has greatly increased. It was once so small we knew the person who committed suicide and the one who was sick with cancer. When the grocer's wife jumped from the top of her building and died, we noticed that the grocer, a talkative man, became quiet, his voice dull. But the neighborhood continued to busy itself with gossip and trade and with current news on the radio that blasted through open windows in summer.

I recall Amram Blau, the head of the anti-Zionist group that called itself Neturei Karta, and who lived in nearby Meah Shearim. I was curious about him, and about anybody with extreme views, and wondered what made them who they were. (I wondered about Moshe Sneh, the head of the Communist party in Israel, what made him who he was.) After the death of his first wife, Amram Blau married a French woman who converted from Christianity to Judaism and who, they say, was as extreme in her views as he was. On my visits to Jerusalem, I've had fantasies about meeting Mrs. Blau, this ultra-religious woman. I'll just go to her house, knock on the door, and she'll invite me in, I'll have a chance to see what she looks like, get to know her. I'll discover what motivated her to marry the leader of Neturei Karta, and to dress modestly covered from head to foot with a long dress and long sleeves and a tight scarf wrapped around her hair, and come to live on a broken-down street, a weary, old neighborhood where houses are crowded, streets are narrow, the air is dark, and everyone is poor.

A street away from my childhood street, a huge yeshiva was built for the followers of a Hasidic dynasty. This yeshiva seems to have been the first of the ultra-religious sects that moved to the north of the city en masse. (The more modern orthodox and secular groups moved to the south of the city.) Friday nights, whenever my uncle visited from America, my father took him there. They returned to the house in wonderment, struck by the rebbe's grand entrance into the praying hall, by how the men in the packed and noisy hall suddenly became silent, separating to make way for the rebbe, who was like Moses parting the Red Sea.

Once multiethnic, my childhood neighborhood is now inhabited almost exclusively by men dressed in black suits and black hats, and women in long dresses, long sleeves, their heads covered with a hat, a wig, a scarf. The streets are buzzing with people, crowds of people shopping for clothes, eating pizza, humus, and falafel in tiny restaurants. People stop to talk with each other, or with beggars, or with shop owners. They are content to be restricted by traditional rules, apart from the secular world, away from the lure of worldly pleasures, away from the influence of nonobservant Jews who profane the Sabbath and dress in ways that reveal the skin.

My friends, mostly secular Jews, condescend to the ultra-religious Jews, seeing them as backward, mirroring Jewish life in Diaspora, and hate them for their attempting to force their restrictions on others. Too many blacks, they say, referring to their black suits. And they don't serve in the army, they add furiously. The religious Jews fear the influence of the secular life on their children. This is a Jewish state, they say, and it should follow the *Halacha* (Jewish law). And no one seems to remember that the hatred between Jewish sects is as old as the second temple, whose destruction is attributed to that very hatred.

There were seeds of a similar feeling, albeit among other groups, when I was growing up—an indifference that we Sabras felt towards anyone who was different from us. Having been born as Jews in Israel, successors of the bold pioneers who built this country, made us feel superior, a superior breed. Our faith in the Zionist vision, in our heroes and leaders, was complete. We aimed at being strong and unyielding. Never again were we going to be victims of a Holocaust, or victims of pogroms described in Bialik's "City of Killings,"

> For the Lord called the Spring and the slaughterer together:
> The sun rose, rye bloomed, and the slaughterer slaughtered[2]

Never again were we going to cry the heart-wrenching plea in Bialik's "On the Slaughter,"

> Sky, have mercy on me!
> If there be in you a God and to that God a path
> and I have not found it—
> you pray for me![3]

We admired these poems and felt the horror they portrayed but we did not identify with the victims. We didn't identify with those who had perished in the Holocaust, those who had been herded, brutalized, and murdered, those who had been humiliated, diminished, and weakened, or those who had survived it. We felt indifferent towards kids our age who had survived the Holocaust, been brought to Israel, and placed mostly in institutions and kibbutzim. We felt indifferent towards the man from Auschwitz with a bewildered face, we thought he didn't belong; and the woman with the number on her arm, we heard she was once skin and bones, we feared her, we did not get close to her. Often the immigrants were taken to a *ma'abarah*, a transitional camp, like the one in the south of Jerusalem, and they were placed in overcrowded and leaky tents. To us it was only a story, not because we did not believe what we heard—we knew it was true—but because we felt distant from every-thing that had happened to the immigrants. The word ma'abarah had a derogatory tone, and we thought the people who lived there had to be inferior. If there was any pity in us it was cold, cold pity.

This, too, has changed with time. It's taken years, but the old generation of Sabras has become less arrogant and more inclusive. The passing of time has humbled us. There are times, perhaps just on brief occasions, when the city, too, sees beyond her strife, gathering religious and secular Jewish children, and until recently Arab children, in her parks, and at the Jerusalem Biblical Zoo. And there are moments when the city harmonizes the sounds of its muezzin calling for prayer, and the pleas of those who pray at the Wailing Wall. There is beauty in the harmony, but also terror, not of the dreadfulness of life, but of its outward gaze like an animal's, "life boundless . . .without regard to its own condition."[4]

There are times when I am like the city, terrified of taking a risk and transforming my life permanently to being free of past constraints. I am divided between remaining as I am—polite, obedient, concerned—and being ruthless, doing what I want, not looking back at my mother, or anyone else whom I left behind. Times when I break through my fear and look beyond obedience, beyond the desire to please others. I think of the Jerusalem that forbade and confined, and yet contained a germ that has helped me connect with the life of the spirit.

I walk on Geulah, the main street. The stores I used to go to no longer exist. My favorite store was the tiny stationery shop owned by a jolly

Hasidic man with a perpetual smile who sold school supplies, candy, and toys and small, lurid booklets containing weekly serial installments of suspenseful love stories, with names such as *Aviva* and *Rachel*, about women and their men. Here I am, by the door of the store, in a light blue jumper with a white shirt, pigtails tied with white ribbons, eagerly buying the new issue, reading it within minutes on my way home, picturing the women in it with voluptuous hips, speaking aggressively. And here I am again on a side street, exchanging books in a small bookstore/library, seeking adventure in books such as *The Deluge* by Henryk Sienkiewicz and *The Good Earth* by Pearl Buck. Across from the bookstore a man sells ice. The street outside his store is always wet. There we buy blocks of ice for our icebox. I am wary of the man. He is impatient, and his face bitter.

I enter the pharmacy where I used to buy soap, hand lotion, and medicine. The owner, a courtly man of Sephardic origin who warmly welcomed his customers, was the only one serving his customers. I can see him standing behind the counter in his white coat, smiling at me and asking how my parents are. I am fourteen years old in my light red summer dress, answering politely, smiling—my mother chided me when I greeted people without a smile, and I always remembered to do so. The people of the neighborhood liked to use the pharmacy phone. We had no phone and there were no public phones on the street. You could use the phone in a store, or the one in the post office in the center of town, which was a long way off. The pharmacy also had a scale on which for a couple of pennies I would weigh myself. Now the pharmacy displays its products, from all over the world, on large, shiny counters. There are many salespeople, all energetic, and the original owner's granddaughter runs the place.

I think of how modest our shops were in the past, how limited our choices were, how prudent we were with our money and possessions, how it never entered our minds that we lacked anything or couldn't afford something we wanted. How we never wanted something we didn't have. Like any other city in Israel, and so many cities around the world, Jerusalem now looks to America as a model. Describing something as "America" means it is good. Consumerism is highly regarded. Material riches are applauded. I remember feeling embarrassed that my father owned part of a building, and now this amuses me. But we lived in a socialist country, and owning property was scorned.

I walk over to Sharabi Street, where I grew up. I am attached to this alley, its simplicity, its audacity to survive. This street has given me a focal place to belong to wherever I am.

I remember Yaffa, a neighbor, whose husband battered her. She would pour gasoline on herself, threatening to set herself on fire—people said it was her way of crying for help. Her daughter Malka, who married a German man, lived one street away. She, too, was battered by her husband. She became sick with cancer and I could hear her scream when I went by her windows, which faced the street. I thought this was the only thing she could do for herself. Isaac, another neighbor, sold motorcycles. He was a rough man who dominated his family. His wife's face was ravaged by agony.

My Sephardic next-door neighbor and her sister attended The Mission, a school run by Christians. There was shame associated with going to a non-Jewish school, especially a Christian one, in a land that prided itself in offering Jewish education. It was rumored that the school attempted to convert the children, and offered financial help to students' families. When people talked about it they whispered. The school was surrounded by walls. Whenever I went by I peeked through the narrow gate, but all I saw was a courtyard, sometimes a few nuns, or a few girls playing.

I go up the stairs to the apartment where I lived. An ultra-religious young woman, plainly dressed, looking weary, opens the door. I tell her who I am. We talk and she tells me she has six children. The apartment is in disarray. The terrace that once basked in the sunlight looks dark, homely. I visit a next-door neighbor, a woman who lived there when I was growing up. Her husband died and her children are grown up. All the way from America, she says in amazement. She is the only Sephardic who still lives on the street. Everyone else is Askenazi. Sephardic Jews, secular Jews, Modern-Orthodox Jews—the people who invited me to their homes to taste their exotic food, to listen to their radio on the Sabbath, people who lent color and truth to the street, no longer live here.

The field I used to play in where we lit bonfires on Lag B'Omer is gone. Gone is the small house on the side of the field. A three-storied building with small windows rises in its stead. There are no gardens, and women no longer chat with each other from their terraces. I stand in the back of the field. I am eleven. We play *kadur hakafa* (a watered down version of baseball). My neighbor friends are here. Boys and girls. We play with a tennis ball. I am good at the game. I am happy. I like catching the ball. Once I catch it and break my pinky. Night falls. We play hide and seek. I hide in one of the gardens, one of my good, earthly gardens.

Walking on Sharabi Street, I remember how every Friday afternoon after polishing the family's shoes I would visit Dina in the Beit Yisrael neighborhood further north to the consternation of my parents, who wanted me to be home to prepare for the Sabbath. I loved her mother's warm greetings. I felt joy there. No one monitored me. Dina's mother would serve me eggplant in tomato sauce and stuffed cabbage. I savored her food. I particularly enjoyed being with Dina before the Sabbath, before being subjected to my family's rigorous Sabbath rules. After our brief visit, Dina would walk me home on the street close to where a suicide bomber recently blew himself up. The street is narrow, ordinary. The neighborhood resonated with unpretentiousness. The houses were unassuming, with humble courtyards. My grandfather, who had come from America in the 1920s, had chosen to live in a house on a street nearby, and for a year, so did my younger son with his wife and daughter. The bomber exploded himself on that unsuspecting street—the one close to where Dina and I walked on—as the Sabbath departed, the sky lit with only a few stars. Many were killed as they were leaving the synagogue there, still wearing their Sabbath clothes.

Dina and I were carefree. Nothing much happened on our walk. We talked, we laughed. When we arrived at my house we reversed our direction and I walked Dina half way back to her house. One time, I remember, when we were fourteen years old, she said she might leave Jerusalem and go and live in a small village on the coast. She wanted to leave home, and sadness seized me at the thought that the distance would prevent us from seeing each other as often as we'd like. We held hands, and her hand was warm, and I thought how much I would miss her.

Sometimes I met Dina on Ben Yehuda Street, in the center of town, to shop, typically for shoes or a bra. I would often see the poet who had translated Tagore into Hebrew, wearing white gloves and a long white dress and carrying a white parasol. Her face was heavily powdered, looking like a nymph or a fairy, unaccountable. Ben Yehuda, a short, hilly street that has always been crowded with shoppers, is now a promenade. There are street performers, musicians, and singers looking for handouts. Dina and I were very picky about the kind of bras we bought, and the kind of sandals we wanted for summer. After we did our shopping we had humus, the best humus in town, we thought, in a restaurant on a side street, off Ben Yehuda.

At the top of the street in a Bohemian café, a jewelry maker, Yossi, had proposed to me on a first date, only hours before Motti proposed. Yossi had visions of us wheeling our baby in a carriage down Ben Yehuda Street. Motti promised me he would be rich. Very rich. He forced a kiss on me. How presumptuous of him to think I would marry him because he would be rich. Yossi promised a trip to England. He attempted to seduce me by telling me that my piano playing was a sublimation of my sexual instincts. When Yossi took me for coffee he showed me how to use the container of sugar, designed to use without a spoon. How worldly he is, I thought. We went to his room. He touched me. He told me I was not a virgin. He thought he could fool me about my own body, my own experiences.

When Mark and I first met, we became frequent customers at Atara, one of our favorite cafés on Ben Yehuda. Across the street was a music store run by a mother and son, where I would shop for sheet music and records. They were German Jews devoted to anything connected to music, and also devoted to each other.

Over the years, the life of Ben Yehuda street had been intermittently shattered. In 1947, the British helped the Arabs plant a bomb-laden truck there, and in the present intifada, several suicide bombers targeted the street. Each bombing casts a pall. The street empties for a while, people stop shopping. But in spite of the grief and the fear, Ben Yehuda gradually shows signs of life again. Before long, the street buzzes with people; performers play their instruments and sing. On our visits to Jerusalem from New York, Mark and I shop there, have humus in a restaurant on a side street. The Bohemian café is gone, and the Arabs and Jews in Jerusalem no longer interact in a friendly way. We despair of ever witnessing an amicable meeting such as the one after the 1967 war between the Arab man who came to my father's store (which was close to Ben Yehuda Street) and embraced my father, and introduced him to his young son.

During my mother's illness, and before I had rented out the store, Dina called to tell me that she saw pigeons flying in through an opening at the top of the shutter that protects the store front. She thought they might be nesting in the store. These pigeons are a bad omen, I thought, symbolic of the city center which was hurt by suicide bombers and has become commercially depressed. I thought they symbolized how the store, once a permanent fixture in the center of town, represented transience, and that the sound of bombs falling silenced my father's modest life's work. To the west of my father's store still stands the Russian Orthodox church in the Russian compound. In the once-parched field is a road and a parking lot, buildings that are part of the Hebrew University, an Israeli court of justice, and a Detention Center. The central prison of Jerusalem that held men of the Jewish underground now houses the Underground Prisoners Museum. An inscription on its door still says "Central Prison Jerusalem" from the British Mandatory period.

Across the street from my father's store was a shop that sold curtains; the space is now inhabited by a toy store. It didn't bother anybody that the owner's wife was a non-Jew. The neighboring shop owners liked her, including my parents. The owner was from Europe and he smoked incessantly. He and my mother would stand by the door of my father's store, chatting, flirting. The talking sometimes annoyed my father, though generally it pleased him when my mother chatted with customers. He would say, That helps my business, but sometimes she overdoes it.

On our summer visits Mark would rent a car and occasionally deliver merchandise for my father or drive him home. Because my father knew only a few words in English and Mark's Hebrew was meager, they spoke in the only language they had in common: German. They were very fond of each other, and conversing in a language neither knew well didn't seem to bother them. My father took pride in knowing every street and alley in the city, and the shortest routes from point to point. But he was a non-driver, oblivious to one-way streets, and he would be angry when Mark didn't follow his driving instructions.

There were more serious conflicts. My father felt hurt and angry any time Mark refused to accompany him to the synagogue on the Sabbath or on a Jewish holiday. Once or twice Mark did go, but the experience tormented him. Because the service was in Hebrew he wasn't able to follow it, and he became resentful. My father insisted that it is all a matter of will. If only Mark would continue to go he would learn to like it. Moreover, Mark's refusal was entirely my fault. My parents agreed on that. They sympathized with the fact that Mark had no knowledge or experience with going to the synagogue because of his non-observant background, but since I did, they said I ought to influence him to go. They were unaware that faith and prayer, the most sacred of all experiences, could be nurtured but never forced, that force does not work.

Recently, during my mother's deteriorated state, I rented the store to a clothing merchant who uses it for storage. I visit it. The store, which once seemed spacious, is narrow. There is a heavy shutter on the door with large padlocks. I remember my father climbing a ladder to get to the upper shelves, close to the ceiling, as meanwhile his helper sat on a small stool by the long counter, dully whiling away his time.

Neighborhoods in the south of the city have changed, too. In Malcha, the old Arab village, a huge new mall has been built. When I go shopping there I see the well-designed houses built on the once-barren hills. In 1960, Mark, who has just arrived in Jerusalem, works on his paintings there in a one-story Arab house—the second floor was destroyed in the 1948 war. The area has been all but laid to waste—you can hear the jackals howl at night. I stand behind Mark, watching him paint, stroking the canvas with his brush. I wear a tight beige skirt and red high-heeled shoes. My hair is cropped. Mark is in jeans and a wide, paint-stained shirt. He is focused on his canvas. I see him stepping back to gain perspective on what he has just done on the canvas, how he makes a choice of colors, how he again and again dips his brush in paint, how he gives birth to a painting. I never saw anyone paint before. I think the process is miraculous. I want to be the backbone of someone involved in such a process, being beside him, believing in him, encouraging him.

After my son moved to Jerusalem in the early 1990s, and especially after my mother became infirm, Mark and I visit Jerusalem three times a year. I shuttle between visiting my mother and visiting with my older son and his family. On the way there or on the way back we often stop in England to visit my younger son and his family. With each visit to Jerusalem I sense the resiliency of the city, how it has been revived time and again from destruction. Everything in my past—the plight of Holocaust survivors and the plight of the Palestinians—acquires more understanding. But while my sympathies have widened, I grieve the new wall built between the Jewish population and the Arab, the slow destruction of hope, the distrust and fear between the two peoples.

I walk in Jerusalem and feel a belonging to the city, however contentious it is. I gaze at the Temple Mount and the mountains that surround it,

> And as in a dream my body remembers:
> crystalline rocks,
> hard-crusted earth,
> a desired
> desert-like air.
>
> Even while I am a thousand miles away
> the body's core belongs here.
> In the center of a flower.
> In the tree from which
> a man hanged himself,
> the trail becoming
> fear and fate[5]

And it belongs in the yearned-for Temple, in the constant memory of the Temple, set apart and sanctified. What would Jerusalem do without that Temple, and the many ancient religions, each striving for and pleading to be first and foremost in the eyes of God? And what would I do without the memory of climbing the hill on my way home from school, the same hill every day, the same street, whose enduring presence delights me, going by Bikkur Cholim Hospital, with the large terrace on its second floor, where patients in white garments look out at the world they hope they will be soon released to. I sit in a café in the Nachalat Shiva, in a neighborhood where Agnon's Isaac, the anti-hero of "Only Yesterday," who is poor and awkward, lived. The neighborhood is no longer inconspicuous. It has boutiques, terraces filled with geraniums, colorful cafés, and restaurants. The surrounding neighborhoods spread, sprawl, extend "the Triangle," the main three roads, parts of which are continuously damaged by suicide bombers and then quickly renovated.

I look back and think of my past prejudices, fears, misperceptions. How little I knew. How often I mistook appearance for reality. I go by the lepers' house in the south of the city, and I enter the abandoned garden and gaze at the abandoned house. It has an aura of a sacred place, set apart, like the tomb of Rachel in Bethlehem, or the tomb of the Patriarchs and Matriarchs in Hebron. I write,

> There was a leper who lived
> in my city on a steeped hill,
> and when we happened in the neighborhood
> we pointed to the direction of his house
> and whispered "leper, leper...."
>
> But in that house someone
> stroked the leper's head,
> and washed him every morning,
> and every evening anointed him with oil.
> And the leper was not afraid of his body.
> He knew he was "worth more than hundreds
> of sparrows." He knew he was worth more than
> his leprous body....

Though we shunned him,
the leper felt like the salt of the earth.
Though we shunned his garden,
the vine and carob trees flourished,
and the cactus grew to a giant size.[6]

The city is still narrow in its vision, even narrower than it was. But it is home. I feel embraced when sharing my memories with people from my past, especially Dina. We spend hours reminiscing, talking, and laughing, sometimes giddily, about our homes, jobs, schools, and the boys and men that crossed our paths.

On this visit I attend a reunion of my army unit in the kibbutz where we served. I remember the wholesome belief we had in the justice of our country, in ourselves as defenders of it, and in our ideals: courage, constancy, loyalty. We didn't know that Joseph Trumpeldor, a national hero who lost his life in a firefight between Shiites and Jews in the north of Palestine in the '20s, did not say "It is good to die for our country," which was attributed to him as his last words, and we repeated with awe. We didn't know Theodor Herzl, the man who envisioned the establishment of the state of Israel for the Jews, whose picture hung on every governmental office wall and in every school, sought far-fetched solutions for the plight of the Jews, among them their conversion to Christianity. But does it matter? These myths embodied the belief in the sanctity of our country, which gave our lives meaning.

On the screen we watch pictures of ourselves in army uniform, the boys muscular and slim, the girls without makeup, natural and simple, smiling. I meet Eitan. Eitan's hair is graying, but he still has a youthful look, body erect, the blue eyes still piercing from behind his glasses. We take a walk. How does he see me? Have I aged terribly? Does my purple hat, which I wear to protect me from the sun, make me look older? I remind him how I once went into his bed when he was sick with a high fever. You are always in my dreams, he says. Remember the shower curtain ring you sent me in the mail when I was in intensive training? he adds. Our young love had, in Proustian words, "its own incomprehensible fatal laws, before our passive and astonished hearts."[7] I think of how Eitan held me when I wept after breaking up with my fiancé as he points to where the dining room used to be, and the carpentry shop, and there is the hut, he says, semi-ruined, in which we once loved, and the grass, now yellowed, that we once lay upon, happy to be.

19

RED HAIR GLISTENING

My mother dies on March 18, 2005, in Jerusalem. I remember once when we visited the Cave of the Machpelah, she leaned on my arm and said, Life leaves in haste. The sky was particularly tender on that visit, like a hand reaching to stroke a dying face.

Before leaving for the funeral home I stand by the van where my mother's body lies. It is a warm day, but I feel an inner chill, and I remain wearing my long winter coat and a woolen hat. A man from the Burial Society approaches me and asks if I want to see my mother. Yes, I say. He lifts the door at the back of the van where I can see my mother's head, and he uncovers her face. I feel numb. My mother looks dead, passing away through her broken remains.

Soon my mother will be dust. Dust to dust. I imagine her small body in a fetal position, bruised from having been dumped into the pit with only a shroud around her. I see myself in the silence of her dust huddling against her thin body, her delicate body, my arm around her thinness, around her bones. We lie like stone, without defenses, in the dust we longed for in our tumultuous hours. Dewdrops of an unperturbed summer inch their way through. The cypress above us endures. The crow that perches on the roof of our old house silences his cawing of sudden terror, covering it with his black wings.

I think of how I trusted you, Mother, to be alive forever, even in your last months, when sometimes you didn't know who I was. I relied on you to trespass your limits for me, if only I asked. If only our hearts had clasped the way our hands did that time, remember? I believed I could always sit by you when you were awake, and when you were sleeping—see the bird you wanted to be. But now this strange, empty space is between us. You said, Vanity, Vanity, this vain world is all Vanity, and you confessed agonizing over minor things. Your yearnings had no beginning and no end. They flooded us. I could never get through them, they were so immense.

Are you a bird now? Free from the heartache over my leaving? Free from shame—you once arrived at the door of a younger brother, having been sent away from your older brother's house (for reasons I don't know). When asked where your suitcase was, you said you had no suitcase, had no other clothes but the dress and the worn underwear you had on. In Jerusalem, many years later, you bought dresses—only cotton, you said, because it breathed—and shoes, and scarves in green and gray and brown, colors that matched your red hair. I liked the way you dressed, without a fuss, a beret in the winter with a colorful pin, and a light, flowery dress in summer, with only a touch of makeup. Father did not understand that you were redeeming yourself, and he was sometimes annoyed at you for "buying so many clothes." But he often remarked that with age you were more beautiful, and with age he loved you more.

Now you are in a realm we on earth know nothing about. I can see you there, becoming smaller and smaller, almost imperceptible. But you do not vanish. Perhaps death is an advent beyond the ocean you had crossed to reach your father, first in America, and after that, in Palestine.

My greatest advocate, my ferocious ally, how strange that you are no longer here. In nursery school you were displeased when you saw me play the triangle in the little orchestra. Why isn't my daughter the conductor? you demanded of the teacher. She is too shy, the teacher replied. You were adamant, Put her there and she won't be shy. At the next performance, the little orchestra played to my hand movements. My heart pounded. I was the conductor, and I was not shy.

Once, on a laundry day, I was sent home from school for talking in class, and was told to bring you back to school. Laundry day was important. In winter the women stood on their terraces the day before, attempting to foresee the next day's weather. On the appointed day, our washerwoman squatted for the entire time, washing sheets and towels. Then you dipped it all in a big basin of boiling water and wrung it. I can still see you leaning down over the terrace railing, hanging the sheets and towels on the line. I don't have strong hands, you would say, and I can't wring the sheets too well. Poor Habiba (the neighbor below us), her courtyard gets wet every time I hang the laundry. I said, You must come back to school with me. Furiously you put on your good clothes, then lipstick, and in a rush took me back. Didn't you talk in class as a child? you asked the headmistress, rhetorically. You reprimanded her for interrupting your laundry day, and for such a trifle!

Your alliance with me continued in high school. You unequivocally defended me against teachers who complained about me disturbing the class by chatting with my friends. I know my daughter, you would say, and if the class was interesting she wouldn't talk. Even when I was an adult you admonished my friends who did not respond to my letter announcing my second summer seminar in Jerusalem. But you did not protect me against your anger. You reprimanded me harshly for disobeying you—the slightest transgression would sometimes anger you. You would stand by Father in his outbursts of anger at me. When it came to me, you and Father stood together. You did not contradict each other, not in my presence. Not when I refused medication—a tablespoon of cod liver oil, or an enema, to strengthen my immune system, or to cure a cold or indigestion. You don't listen, you would say with extreme frustration, regardless of whether the wrongdoing was major or minor. When I was a child of four you spanked me for not eating the grapes you gave me. I cried. You put me on your lap and kissed me, your eyes and mouth drooped slightly, remorsefully. Then, with a smile, you held me closer.

I watched you cook, or helped you clean up. The kitchen was our sanctuary, a place where we bonded, sometimes tenderly. When I was six I remember that

> On a small stool in the kitchen I stood
> kneading ground fish into patties.
> I was not good at this.
> You said I was not practical.

Dense heat in summer days,
evenings, drafts through open windows,
the chilling finger you shook at me,
drove me away.
I learned to feel and think alone,
a reed uprooted from mud.

The wind does what it wants
now still, now harsh.
An orphaned girl, shamed and proud,
your fate takes leave to an untold world.

Are you Heaven's daughter now?
No, not a daughter,
but a song unsung,
a spirit
in all substances,
earth,
worms,
the universe itself.

It is only in sickness and in death
that I wanted to huddle against you,
put my arm around your thin bones,
as if through touching your mellowing end
you will be yourself,
and I, the reed I was,
rooted in your gentle garden.[1]

Once, back from the army, while sitting in the kitchen, you asked me
whether Eitan and I had kissed. You were curious, there was nothing
intrusive about the question, it was part of the intimate conversations
we had. Another time you advised me not to marry David—subtly, as
an aside, leaving me free to do as I wish. Your displeasure with Tzvi for
not wearing a yarmulke was a long-forgotten occurrence. On several
occasions you told me intimate things about yourself: I was at a wedding

in Tel Aviv, you once said, and a man invited me to dance. We danced and danced. As you talked I could see you dancing: you are nimble, your small, trim figure moving eloquently to the music, your head tilted a bit to the side, red hair glistening, and you are smiling. The next day, you continued, I was window shopping, and there was that same man beside me, saying hello. It was a surprise. I didn't look as well as I looked at the wedding. I wore an ordinary dress, not the blue one, of course, I had worn at the wedding, and my face wasn't made up. I was tired, and I think I looked haggard. You told me you were sad. You must have thought the man was disappointed in the way you looked. In one day the bit of happiness you had given yourself was stolen.

There were also your quasi-mysterious comings and goings. You would say, I am going to visit the rabbi. You looked pressed, your mouth protruding, your eyes forward. There was something on your mind you needed to discuss. You didn't tell me what it was. From the terrace I could see you turning onto the street that went up the hill leading to the rabbi's home. A treeless street, the houses without gardens. Your walk was brisk. You returned an hour later. An air of calm and reassurance about you, and you would say, I also talked to the rabbi's wife, she is a very bright woman. It gives me rest, happiness, that you have your own life. A similar aura of calm surrounded you upon your return from the Mikvah. You are in a loose dress. Your hair is wet. You have had a few moments for yourself, and you are relaxed. You go about the chores in the house with more quietude than usual.

I am looking at the dark river from my window in New York. It is 10:20 p.m. and I just came back from synagogue where they hold an evening service every night. In my simple, unpretentious shul, I say Kaddish for you, Mother—I recite the mysterious Aramaic prayer that traverses space and time and brings me closer to you. Secular life has proven insufficient. It is too much in love with matter. The Kaddish sanctifies, and glorifies, and praises, and blesses, and extols, and lauds the name of the Holy One. I am committed to saying it. This surprises me. It may surprise you too.

Notes

Overture: Terror and Ice Cream

1. Cavafy, C.P. From "Growing in Spirit." In *Collected Poems*, trans. Edmund Keeley & Philip Sherrard, ed. George Savidis. Princeton, New Jersey: Princeton University Press, 1975, page 176.

2. Rilke, Rainer Maria. From "The Notebooks of Malte Laurids Brigge," (The Prodigal Son). In *The Selected Poetry of Rainer Maria Rilke*, trans. and ed. Stephen Mitchell. New York, New York: Vintage Books, A Division of Random House, 1984, page 109.

3. Ibid., page 107.

Chapter 11: Giving Birth

1. Miriam, Rivka. From "Never Will I Be Like the Mother in the Picture." In *These Mountains: Selected Poems of Rivka Miriam*, trans. Linda Stern Zisquit. New Milford, Connecticut: The Toby Press, 2009, page 51.

2. Dhalla, Maneckji Nusservanji, ed. and trans. From "Khordah Avesta," Part I. In *The Nyaishes or Zoroastrian Litanies*. New York: AMS Press Inc., 1965, page 9.

3. Hung, William. From "Chiang Village (three poems)." In *Tu Fu, China's Greatest Poet*. New York: Russell & Russell, 1969, page 115.

4. Bonhoeffer, Dietrich. From *Letters and Papers from Prison*, ed. Eberhard Bethge. New York, New York: The Macmillan Company, 1972, page 53.

Chapter 12: Awakening

1. Ady, Endre. From "The Chastity Belt." In *Poems of Endre Ady*, trans. Anton N. Nyerges. Buffalo, New York: Hungarian Cultural Foundation, 1972, page 299.

2. Ady, Endre. From "Psalm of Night." In *Poems of Endre Ady*, trans. Anton N. Nyerges. Buffalo, New York: Hungarian Cultural Foundation, 1969, page 277.

3. Plato, *The Symposium*, trans. Walter Hamilton. City of Westminster, London: Penguin Books, 1951, page 61.

4. Ibid., page 65.

5. Proust, Marcel. From "Swann's Way." *Remembrance of Things Past*, Vol. 1, trans. C.K. Scott Moncrieff and Terence Kilmartin. New York, New York: Random House, 1981, page 89.

Chapter 13: "I Have No World But One"

1. Bialik, Hayim Nahman. From "The Sea of Silence." In *Songs From Bialik: Selected Poems of Hayim Nahman Bialik*, ed. and trans. Atar Hadari. Syracuse, New York: Syracuse University Press, 2000, page 36.

2. Simpson, Louis. From "My Father in the Night Commanding No." In *At the End of the Open Road*. Middletown, Connecticut: Wesleyan University Press, 1960, page 37.

3. Berghash, Rachel. From "A Small Man Is Greater Than A Starry Dome." In *Chicago Review*, Volume 36, Number 2, 1988.

4. Berghash, Rachel. From "Conception," In *Pulp*, Vol. 7, Number 1, 1981.

5. Berghash, Rachel. From an unpublished poem, "Landing in Motherland."

6. Ludwig Wittgenstein, *Tractatus Logico-Philosophicus*, trans. D.F. Pears & B.F. McGuinness. Atlantic Highlands, New Jersey: The Humanities Press, 1961, page 73.

7. Berghash, Rachel. "Carob Pods," *West Wind Review*. In *The Sixteenth Anthology*, 1997.

Chapter 14: The Sun Setting on the Hudson River

1. Berghash, Rachel. From an unpublished poem, "The Visit."

2. Luzzatto, Moshe Chayim, *The Path of the Just*, trans. Shraga Silverstien. Boys Town Jerusalem and Yaakov Feldheim: 1966, page 283.

3. Whitehead, Alfred North, *Religion in the Making*. New York, New York: The World Publishing Company, 1973, page 86.

4. Heaney, Seamus. From "Station Island, # VI." In *Station Island*. New York, New York: Farrar, Straus, Giroux, 1985, page 76.

5. Milosz. Czeslaw. From "Father Ch., Many Years Later." In *Unattainable Earth*, translated by the author and Robert Hass. New York, New York: The Ecco Press, 1986, page 91.

6. Milosz. Czeslaw. From "Consciousness." In *Unattainable Earth*, translated by the author and Robert Hass. New York, New York: The Ecco Press, 1986, page 74.

Chapter 15: Apples Dipped in Honey

1. Buber, Martin. *Tales of the Hasidim, Early Masters*, trans. Olga Marx. New York, New York: Schocken Books, 1970, page 182.

2. Berghash, Rachel. From an unpublished poem, "Figs."

3. Rilke, Rainer Maria. From "The Tenth Elegy." In *The Selected Poetry of Rainer Maria Rilke*, ed. and trans. Stephen Mitchell. New York: Vintage Books, A Division of Random House, 1984, page 205.

4. Whitehead, Alfred North, *Religion in the Making*. New York, New York: The World Publishing Company, 1973, page 115.

5. Rilke, Rainer Maria. From "The Fourth Elegy." In *The Selected Poetry of Rainer Maria Rilke*, ed. and trans. Stephen Mitchell. New York, New York: Vintage Books, A Division of Random House, 1984, page 173.

6. Proust, Marcel. From "Swann's Way." In *Remembrance of Things Past*, Vol. 1, trans. C.K. Scott Moncrieff and Terence Kilmartin. New York, New York: Random House, 1981, page 68.

Chapter 17: Mother and Motherland

1. Nicholson, R.A. From "The Meditations of Ma'arri." In *Studies in Islamic Poetry*. London, England: Cambridge University Press, 1969, page 108.

2. Berghash, Rachel. From "Jericho." In *Israel Horizons*, Volume 43, No.4, Winter, 1995/96.

3. Buber, Martin. *Tales of the Hasidim, Early Masters,* trans. Olga Marx. New York, New York: Schocken Books, 1970, page 186.

4. Berghash, Rachel. From "The Goat, 1945." In *Bridges, A Jewish Feminist Journal,* Vol. 13, No. 2, Autumn, 2008.

Chapter 18: The Terrace That Basked in the Sunlight

1. Keeley, Edmund. From an unpublished note, 1907. In *Cavafy's Alexandria, Study of a Myth in Progress.* Cambridge, Massachusetts: Harvard University Press, 1976, page 19.

2. Bialik, Hayim Nahman. From "City of Killings." In *Songs From Bialik: Selected Poems of Hayim Nahman Bialik,* ed. and trans. Atar Hadari. Syracuse: Syracuse University Press, 2000, page 1.

3. Bialik, Hayim Nahman. From "On the Slaughter." In *Songs From Bialik: Selected Poems of Hayim Nahman Bialik,* ed. and trans. Atar Hadari. Syracuse: Syracuse University Press, 2000, page 11.

4. Rilke, Rainer Maria. From "The Eighth Elegy." In *The Selected Poetry of Rainer Maria Rilke,* ed. and trans. Stephen Mitchell. New York, New York: Vintage Books, A Division of Random House, 1984, page 195.

5. Berghash, Rachel. From an unpublished poem, "Landscape of Wild Tears."

6. Berghash, Rachel. From "Like the Salt of the Earth." In *The Psychoanalytic Perspectives,* Vol. 3, Number 1, Fall/Winter, 2005.

7. Proust, Marcel. From "Swann's Way." *Remembrance of Things Past,* Vol. 1, trans. C.K. Scott Moncrieff and Terence Kilmartin. New York, New York: Random House, 1981, page 214.

Chapter 19: Red Hair Glistening

1. Berghash, Rachel. Unpublished poem, "In Your Gentle Garden."

Bibliography

Agnon, Shmuel Yosef. *Only Yesterday,* trans. Barbara Harshav. Princeton, New Jersey: Princeton University Press, 2000.

Be'er, Haim. "King of the Art 'From Himself:' Profile of the First Artist in Eretz Yisrael." *Ha'aretz,* 5/18/79, pages 25-26.

Chang, Garma C.C., translator and annotator. *The Hundred Thousand Songs of Milarepa,* Volumes I and II. New Hyde Park: University Books, 1962.

Dawn-Samdup, Lama Kazi. Edited with Introduction and Annotations by W.Y. Evans-Wentz, *Tibet's Great Yogi Milarepa.* London, England: Oxford University Press, 1965.

Halberstam Mandelbaum, Yitta. *Holy Brother, Inspiring Stories and Enchanted Tales about Rabbi Shlomo Carlebach.* Northvale, New Jersey, Jerusalem: Jason Aronson Inc., 1997.

Moore, G.E. *"Principia Ethica,"* London, England: Cambridge University Press, 1965.

Saint John of the Cross. *The Complete Works of Saint John of the Cross,* trans. and ed. E. Allison Peers. Westminster, Maryland: The Newman Press, 1964.

Saint Teresa of Jesus. *The Complete Works of Saint Teresa of Jesus,* trans. and ed. E. Allison Peers. London and New York: Sheed & Ward, 1957.

Acknowledgments

Portions from this book, in different versions, were published in:

Crab Orchard Review, Vol. 8, No.2, 2003.

WBAI Newsletter, 1987; trans. into Hebrew by the author, *Hadoar,* January 27, 1989.

Deep gratitude to my editor, Ruth Greenstein, for her insights and invaluable input; to Katherine Jillson for her constant, generous help; to Jonathan Brand for his backing and suggestions; to my husband, Mark, for being there along the way; and to my children, my grandchildren, and my friends, for being who they are.

$4 — Gen 8/10 K

CPSIA information can be obtained at www.ICGtesting.com
Printed in the USA
LVOW061912011112

305451LV00009B/25/P